Writing for Journalists

Writing for Journalists is about the craft of journalistic writing: how to put one word after another so that the reader gets the message, or the joke, goes on reading and comes back for more. It is a practical guide for all those who write for publication in newspapers and periodicals, whether students, trainees or professionals.

Writing for Journalists introduces the reader to the essentials of good writing. Based on critical analysis of news stories, features and reviews from daily and weekly newspapers, consumer magazines and specialist trade journals, *Writing for Journalists* includes:

- advice on how to start writing and how to improve and develop your style
- how to write a news story which is informative, concise and readable
- tips on feature writing, from profiles to product round-ups
- how to research, structure and write reviews
- a glossary of journalistic terms and suggestions for further reading

Wynford Hicks is a freelance journalist and editorial trainer. He is the author of *English for Journalists*, now in its second edition.

Writing for Journalists

Wynford Hicks

with Sally Adams and Harriett Gilbert

London and New York

First published 1999 by Routledge
11 New Fetter Lane, London EC4P 4EE

Simultaneously published in the USA and Canada
by Routledge
29 West 35th Street, New York, NY 10001

Typeset in Goudy Oldstyle by Keystroke, Jacaranda Lodge, Wolverhampton
Printed and bound in Great Britain by TJ International Ltd, Padstow, Cornwall

British Library Cataloguing in Publication Data
A catalogue record for this book is available from the British Library.

Library of Congress Cataloguing in Publication Data
A catalogue record for this book has been requested.

ISBN 0–415–18444–4 (hbk)
    0–415–18445–2 (pbk)

Contents

Contributors

Wynford Hicks is a freelance journalist and editorial trainer. He has worked as a reporter, sub-editor, feature writer, editor and editorial consultant for newspapers, books and magazines and as a teacher of journalism specialising in sub-editing, writing styles and the use of English. He is the author of *English for Journalists*, now in its second edition.

Sally Adams is a writer, editor and lecturer. She has worked as deputy editor of *She*, editor of *Mother and Baby* and *Weight Watchers Magazine*, as a reporter on the *Christchurch Press*, New Zealand, and as the letters page editor on the *San Francisco Chronicle*. She has written for the *Guardian*, *Daily Mail*, *Company*, *Evening Standard* and *Good Housekeeping*. She is a visiting tutor at the London College of Fashion.

Harriett Gilbert is a novelist, broadcaster and journalist. She was literary editor of the *New Statesman* and has written books and arts reviews for, among others, *Time Out*, the *Listener* and the *Independent*. She presents the *Meridian Books* programme for BBC World Service Radio and is a regular arts reviewer on Radios 3 and 4. She lectures in journalism at City University.

Acknowledgements

The authors and publisher would like to thank all those journalists whose work we have quoted to illustrate the points made in this book. In particular we would like to thank the following for permission to reprint material:

'McDonald's the winner and loser'
Ian Cobain, *Daily Mail*, 20 June 1997

'Parson's course record puts pressure on Woods'
Daily Telegraph, 14 February 1997

'Man killed as L-drive car plunges off cliff'
© Telegraph Group Ltd, London, 1998. With thanks to Sean O'Neill.

'Abbey overflows for Compton'
Reproduced with permission of the *Guardian*

'Picnic in the bedroom'
Janet Harmer, *Caterer and Hotelkeeper*, 11 June 1998
Reproduced with the permission of the Editor of *Caterer and Hotelkeeper*

'I love the job but do I have to wear that hat?'
Kerry Fowler, *Good Housekeeping*, June 1998
Reproduced with permission from *Good Housekeeping*, June 1998

Review of *The Whereabouts of Eneas McNulty*
Used with the permission of Adam Mars-Jones

Review of *From the Choirgirl Hotel*
Sylvia Patterson © *Frank*/Wagadon Ltd

1
Introduction

WHAT THIS BOOK IS

This book is about the craft of journalistic writing: putting one word after another so that the reader gets the message – or the joke – goes on reading and comes back for more. Good writing is essential to journalism: without it, important news, intriguing stories, insight and analysis, gossip and opinion could not reach their potential audience.

Writing can also be a pleasure in itself: finding the right word, getting it to fit together with other words in a sentence, constructing a paragraph that conveys meaning and creates delight . . . There is pride in a well-written piece, in the positive feedback from editors, readers, fellow journalists.

This book is a practical guide for those who write for publication in newspapers and periodicals, whether they are students, trainees or more experienced people. Though aimed at professionals, it should also be useful to those who write as a hobby, for propaganda purposes – or because they have a passionate love of writing.

WHAT THIS BOOK IS NOT

But this is not a book *about* journalism. It does not set out to survey the field, to describe the various jobs that journalists do in newspapers and magazines. And it is not an introduction to new or radical forms of journalism – multimedia, the alternative press, the constantly developing world of the Internet. Thus it is not a careers guide for would-be journalists.

Nor is it a review of the issues in journalism. It does not discuss privacy or bias or the vexed question of the ownership of the press. It does not try to answer the question: is journalism in decline? Thus it is unlikely to be adopted as a media studies textbook.

It does not specifically cover broadcast journalism, though many of the points made also apply to TV and radio writing. It does not give detailed guidance on specialised areas such as sport, fashion, consumer and financial journalism. And it does not, except in passing, tell you how to find stories, do research or interview people.

Though sub-editors – and trainee subs – should find it useful as a guide to rewriting, it does not pretend to be a sub's manual. It does not tell you how to cut copy, write headlines or check proofs. It does not cover editing, design, media law . . .

We make no apology for this. In our view writing is the key journalistic skill without which everything else would collapse. That is why we think it deserves a book of its own.

WHO CARES WHETHER JOURNALISTIC WRITING IS ANY GOOD OR NOT?

This may look like a silly question: surely all journalists, particularly editors, aspire to write well themselves and publish good writing? Alas, apparently, not.

The experience of some graduates of journalism courses in their first jobs is that much of what they learnt at college is neither valued nor even wanted by their editors and senior colleagues.

Of course, this might mean that what was being taught at college, instead of being proper journalism, was some kind of ivory-tower non-sense – but the evidence is all the other way. British journalism courses (as opposed to the media studies ones) are responsive to industry demands, vetted by professional training bodies – and taught by journalists.

The problem is that many editors and senior journalists don't seem to bother very much about whether their publications are well written – or even whether they are in grammatically correct English. As Harry Blamires wrote in his introduction to *Correcting your English*, a collection of mistakes published in newspapers and magazines:

Readers may be shocked, as indeed I was myself, to discover the sheer quantity of error in current journalism. They may be astonished to find how large is the proportion of error culled from the quality press and smart magazines. Assembling the bad sentences together en masse brings home to us that we have come to tolerate a shocking degree of slovenliness and illogicality at the level of what is supposed to be educated communication.

It's true that some of what Blamires calls 'error' is conscious colloquialism but most of his examples prove his point: that many editors don't seem to bother very much about the quality of the writing they publish.

Others, on the other hand, do. There is some excellent writing published in British newspapers and periodicals. And it is clear that it can help to bring commercial success.

The *Daily Mail* consistently outsells the *Daily Express* for all sorts of reasons. One of them is the overall quality and professionalism of the writing in the *Mail*. The *Express* may have some good individual writers but as a package it fails to deliver.

The *Spectator* has established a reputation for good writing while its main rival, the *New Statesman*, has been rescued and rethought, refocused politically and journalistically, redesigned and relaunched, more often than any publication in periodical publishing history – but has remained an effort to read. The result is that not that many people read it.

To many, the greatest era of the *Sunday Times* was in the 1970s when Harold Evans, in shirtsleeves, edited on Saturday nights as well as planning strategy throughout the week. The whole paper, including the colour magazine, bore his stamp. Good writers – staff and freelance – were carefully edited to ensure that the finished product was crisp and stylish.

Evans has long gone and with him the paper's reputation for radical investigative journalism – but the general standard of the writing remains good. The *Sunday Times* continues to dominate its sector of the market not merely by publishing more and heavier sections than its competitors, not merely by having a few stars such as A A Gill, but by being consistently readable.

Over at the *Guardian*, there is a different approach. Traditionally a 'writer's paper', where talented individuals are encouraged but subediting is not highly rated, it publishes some of the best pieces in British journalism as well as some of the worst (for example, clumsy, convoluted news stories with intros that go on for ever).

But the best are very good – lively, thought-provoking, up-to-the-minute. Over a generation the *Guardian* has transformed itself from a stuffy, provincial, nonconformist (in the Christian sense), liberal/Liberal newspaper into a bright, metropolitan, trendy (in every sense), critical New Labour one.

Once there was a *Guardian* reader – educated, concerned, radical, interested in the arts . . . Now there are all sorts of *Guardian* readers, and the paper's cunning mix is designed to cater to them all – and still go looking for new ones. But the voice is often distinctive, and much of the writing is very good indeed.

The *Independent*, by contrast, has failed to develop its own distinctive voice – indeed all too often it has been turgid and a great effort to read. Just as the *Guardian* was abandoning worthiness per se, the *Independent* insisted on taking it up. Then, having noticed that it wasn't publishing any jokes, the *Independent* hired the celebrated comic writer Miles Kington – but at his best he has tended to make the rest of the paper seem even duller. And, as with the *Statesman*, each revamp is a sign of increasing desperation.

Can anybody doubt that many people prefer the *Guardian* to the *Independent*, the *Spectator* to the *New Statesman*, the *Mail* to the *Express*, at least partly because they enjoy good writing?

So if you're a trainee journalist in an office where good writing is not valued, do not despair. Do the job you're doing as well as you can – and get ready for your next one. The future is more likely to be yours than your editor's.

CAN WRITING BE TAUGHT?

This is the wrong question – unless you're a prospective teacher of journalism. The question, if you're a would-be journalist (or indeed any kind of writer), is: can writing be *learnt*?

And the answer is: of course it can, providing that you have at least some talent and – what is more important – that you have a lot of determination and are prepared to work hard.

If you want to succeed as a writer, you must be prepared to read a lot, finding good models and learning from them; you must be prepared to think imaginatively about readers and how they think and feel rather than luxuriate inside your own comfortable world; you must be prepared to take time practising, experimenting, revising.

You must be prepared to listen to criticism and take it into account while not letting it get on top of you. You must develop confidence in your own ability but not let it become arrogance.

This book makes all sorts of recommendations about how to improve your writing but it cannot tell you how much progress you are likely to make. It tries to be helpful and encouraging but it does not pretend to be diagnostic. And – unlike those gimmicky writing courses advertised to trap the vain, the naive and the unwary – it cannot honestly 'guarantee success or your money back'.

GETTING DOWN TO WRITING

Make a plan before you start

Making a plan before you start to write is an excellent idea, even if you keep it in your head. And the longer and more complex the piece, the more there is to be gained from setting the plan down on paper – or on the keyboard.

Of course you may well revise the plan as you go, particularly if you start writing before your research is completed. But that is not a reason for doing without a plan.

Write straight on to the keyboard

Unless you want to spend your whole life writing, which won't give you much time to find and research stories – never mind going to the pub or practising the cello – don't bother with a handwritten draft. Why introduce an unnecessary stage into the writing process?

Don't use the excuse that your typing is slow and inaccurate. First, obviously, learn to touch-type, so you can write straight on to the keyboard at the speed at which you think. For most people this will be about 25 words a minute – a speed far slower than that of a professional copy typist.

(There's a key distinction here between the skills of typing and shorthand. As far as writing is concerned, there's not much point in learning to type faster than 25wpm: accuracy is what counts. By contrast, with shorthand the speeds that most journalist students and trainees reach if they work hard, typically 80–100wpm, are of limited use in getting down extensive quotes of normal speech. Shorthand really comes into its own above 100wpm.)

Even if you don't type very well, you should avoid the handwritten draft stage. After all, the piece is going to end up typed – presumably by you. So get down to it straightaway, however few fingers you use.

Write notes to get started

Some people find the act of writing difficult. They feel inhibited from starting to write, as though they were on the high diving board or the top of a ski run.

Reporters don't often suffer from this kind of writer's block because, assuming they have found a story in the first place, the task of writing an intro for it is usually a relatively simple one. Note: not easy but simple, meaning that reporters have a limited range of options; they are not conventionally expected to invent, to be 'creative'.

One reason why journalists should start as reporters is that it's a great way to get into the habit of writing.

However, if you've not yet acquired the habit and tend to freeze at the keyboard, don't just sit there agonising. Having written your basic plan, add further headings; enumerate, list, illustrate. Don't sweat over the first paragraph: begin somewhere in the middle; begin with something you know you're going to include – an anecdote, a quote – knowing you can reposition it later. Get started, knowing that on the word processor you're not committed to your first draft.

Revise, revise

Always leave yourself time to revise what you have written. Even if you're writing news to a tight deadline, try to spend a minute or two looking over your story. And if you're a feature writer or reviewer, revision is an essential part of the writing process.

If you're lucky, a competent sub-editor will check your copy before it goes to press, but that is no reason to pretend to yourself that you are not responsible for what you write. As well as looking for the obvious – errors of fact, names wrong, spelling and grammar mistakes, confusion caused by bad punctuation – try to read your story from the reader's point of view. Does it make sense in their terms? Is it clear? Does it really hit the target?

Master the basics

You can't start to write well without having a grasp of the basics of English usage such as grammar, spelling and punctuation. To develop a journalistic style you will need to learn how to use quotes, to handle reported speech, to choose the right word from a variety of different ones. When should you use foreign words and phrases, slang, jargon – and what about clichés? What is 'house style'? And so on.

The basics of English and journalistic language are covered in a companion volume, *English for Journalists*. In this book we have in general tried not to repeat material included in the first.

DIFFERENT KINDS OF JOURNALISM

There are obviously different kinds of journalism – thus different demands on the journalist as writer. Conventionally, people distinguish in market-sector terms between newspapers and periodicals, tabloid and broadsheet newspapers, and so on.

Some of these conventional assumptions can be simplistic when applied to the way journalism is written. For example, a weekly trade periodical is in fact a newspaper. In its approach to news writing it has as much in common with other weeklies – local newspapers, say, or Sunday newspapers – as it does with monthly trade periodicals. Indeed 'news' in monthly publications is not the same thing at all.

Second, while everybody goes on about the stylistic differences between tabloids and broadsheets, less attention is paid to those between middle-market tabloids, such as the *Mail*, and downmarket tabloids, such as the *Sun*. Whereas features published by the *Guardian* are sometimes reprinted by the *Mail* (and vice versa) with no alterations to the text, most *Mail* features would not fit easily into the *Sun*.

Third, in style terms there are surprising affinities that cross the conventional divisions. For example, the *Sun* and the *Guardian* both include more jokes in the text and punning headlines than the *Mail* does.

Fourth, while *Guardian* stories typically have longer words, sentences and paragraphs than those in the *Mail*, which are in turn longer than those in the *Sun*, it does not follow, for example, that students and trainees who want to end up on the *Guardian* should practise writing at great length.

Indeed our advice to students and trainees is not to begin by imitating the style of a particular publication – or even a particular type of publication. Instead we think you should try to develop an effective writing style by learning from the various good models available. We think that – whoever you are – you can learn from good newspapers and periodicals, broadsheets and tabloids, dailies, weeklies and monthlies.

This book does not claim to give detailed guidance on all the possible permutations of journalistic writing. Instead we take the old-fashioned view that journalism students and trainees should gain a basic all-round competence in news and feature writing.

Thus we cover the straight news story and a number of variations, but not foreign news as such, since trainees are unlikely to find themselves being sent to Algeria or Bosnia. Also, as has already been said, we do not set out to give detailed guidance on specialist areas such as financial and sports reporting. In features we concentrate on the basic formats used in newspapers, consumer magazines and the trade press.

We include a chapter on reviewing because it is not a branch of feature writing but a separate skill, which is in great demand. Reviews in newspapers and periodicals are written by all sorts of journalists including juniors and 'experts' who often start with little experience of writing for publication.

We have taken examples from a wide range of publications but we repeat: our intention is not to 'cover the field of journalism'. In newspapers we have often used examples from the nationals rather than regional or local papers because they are more familiar to readers and easier to get hold of. In periodicals, too, we have tended to use the bigger, better-known titles.

STYLE

In the chapters that follow the different demands of writing news, features and reviews are discussed separately. In the final chapter we look at style as such. We review what the experts have said about the principles of good journalistic writing and suggest how you can develop an effective style.

For whatever divides the different forms of journalism there is such a thing as a distinctive journalistic approach to writing. Journalism – at least in the Anglo-Saxon tradition – is informal rather than formal; active rather than passive; a temporary, inconclusive, ad hoc, interim reaction rather than a definitive, measured statement.

Journalists always claim to deliver the latest – but never claim to have said or written the last word.

Journalism may be factual or polemical, universal or personal, laconic or ornate, serious or comic, but on top of the obvious mix of information and entertainment its stock in trade is shock, surprise, contrast. That is why journalists are always saying 'BUT', often for emphasis at the beginning of sentences.

All journalists tell stories, whether interesting in themselves or used to grab the reader's attention or illustrate a point. Journalists almost always prefer analogy (finding another example of the same thing) to analysis (breaking something down to examine it).

Journalists – in print as well as broadcasting – use the spoken word all the time. They quote what people say to add strength and colour to observation and they often use speech patterns and idioms in their writing.

Journalists are interpreters between specialist sources and the general public, translators of scientific jargon into plain English, scourges of obfuscation, mystification, misinformation. Or they should be.

A good journalist can always write a story short even if they would prefer to have the space for an expanded version. Thus the best general writing exercise for a would-be journalist is what English teachers call the precis or summary, in which a prose passage is reduced to a prescribed length. Unlike the simplest form of sub-editing, in which whole paragraphs are cut from a story so that its style remains unaltered, the precis involves condensing and rewriting as well as cutting.

Journalists have a confused and ambivalent relationship with up-to-date slang, coinages, trendy expressions. They are always looking for new, arresting ways of saying the same old things – but they do more than anybody else to ensure that the new quickly becomes the familiar. Thus good journalists are always trying (and usually failing) to avoid clichés.

Politicians, academics and other people who take themselves far too seriously sometimes criticise journalism for being superficial. In other words, they seem to be saying, without being deep it is readable. From the writing point of view this suggests that it has hit the target.

2
Writing news

WHAT IS NEWS?

News is easy enough to define. To be news, something must be factual, new and interesting.

There must be facts to report – without them there can be no news. The facts must be new – to your readers at least. And these facts must be likely to interest your readers.

'News is something that somebody somewhere doesn't want you to print/wants to suppress. All the rest is advertising.'
Attributed to William Randolph Hearst and Lord Northcliffe

So if a historian makes a discovery about the eating habits of the Ancient Britons, say, somebody can write a news story about it for the specialist periodical *History Today*. The information will be new to its readers, though the people concerned lived hundreds of years ago. Then, when the story is published, it can be followed up by a national newspaper like the *Daily Telegraph* or the *Sunday Mirror*, on the assumption that it would appeal to their readers.

Being able to identify what will interest readers is called having a news sense. There are all sorts of dictums about news (some of which contradict others): that bad news sells more papers than good news; that news is what somebody wants to suppress; that readers are most interested in events and issues that affect them directly; that news is essentially about people; that readers want to read about people like themselves; that readers are, above all, fascinated by the lives, loves and scandals of the famous . . .

It may sound cynical but the most useful guidance for journalism students and trainees is probably that news is what's now being published on the news pages of newspapers and magazines. In other words, whatever the guides and textbooks may say, what the papers actually say is more important.

'News is what a chap who doesn't care much about anything wants to read. And it's only news until he's read it. After that it's dead.'
    Evelyn Waugh in *Scoop*

Some commentators have distinguished between 'hard' news about 'real', 'serious', 'important' events affecting people's lives and 'soft' news about 'trivial' incidents (such as a cat getting stuck up a tree and being rescued by the fire brigade). Those analysing the content of newspapers for its own sake may find this distinction useful, but in terms of journalistic style it can be a dead end. The fact is that there is no clear *stylistic* distinction between 'hard' and 'soft' news writing.

It makes more sense to say that there is a mainstream, traditional approach to news writing – with a number of variants. The reporter may use one of these variants – the narrative style, say – to cover the rescue of a cat stuck up a tree or the siege of Sarajevo. Or they may decide, in either case, to opt for the traditional approach. In fact both 'hard' and 'soft' news can be written either way.

Since we're talking definitions, why is a news report called a 'story'? Elsewhere, the word means anecdote or narrative, fiction or fib – though only a cynic would say that the last two definitions tell the essential truth about journalism.

In fact the word 'story' applied to a news report emphasises that it is a construct, something crafted to interest a reader (rather than an unstructured 'objective' version of the facts). In some ways the word is misleading since, as we shall see, a traditional news story does not use the narrative style.

And, while we're at it, what is an 'angle'? As with 'story' the dictionary seems to provide ammunition for those hostile to journalism. An angle is 'a point of view, a way of looking at something (*colloq*); a scheme, a plan devised for profit (*slang*)', while to angle is 'to present (news, etc.) in such a way as to serve a particular end' (*Chambers Dictionary*).

'When a dog bites a man, that is not news, because it happens so often. But if a man bites a dog, that is news.'
    Attributed to John B Bogart and Charles Dana

We can't blame the dictionary for jumbling things together but there is a key distinction to be made between having a way of looking at something (essential if sense is to be made of it) and presenting news to serve a particular purpose (propaganda). Essentially, a news angle comes from the reporter's interpretation of events – which they invite the reader to share.

The reporter who wrote this intro was clearly amazed by what had happened:

> Former Cabinet minister Cecil Parkinson made an astonishing return to front-line politics today when new Tory leader William Hague appointed him party chairman.
> London *Evening Standard*

By contrast, the reporter who wrote this one had plenty of time to see it coming:

> McDonald's won a hollow victory over two Green campaigners yesterday after the longest libel trial in history.
> *Daily Mail*

In both cases the reporter has a clear idea of what the story is. Advocates of 'objective' journalism may criticise this reporting from a point of view – but nowadays all national papers do it, including the *Guardian*:

> Victims of the world's worst *E coli* food poisoning outbreak reacted furiously last night after the Scottish butcher's shop which sold contaminated meat was fined just £2,250.
> *Guardian*

That 'just' shows clearly what the reporter thinks of the fine. 'Comment is free, but facts are sacred' (*Guardian* editor C P Scott, 1921) may still be the paper's motto but nobody would claim that their news stories were written without an angle.

A QUICK WORD BEFORE YOU START

It's not original to point out that news journalism is all about questions: the ones you ask yourself before you leave the office or pick up the phone; the ones you ask when you're interviewing and gathering material – above all, the ones your reader wants you to answer.

Begin with the readers of your publication. You need to know who they are, what they're interested in, what makes them tick. (For more on this see 'Writing features', page 51.)

Then what's the story about? In some cases – a fire, say – the question answers itself. In others – a complicated fraud case – you may have to wrestle with the material to make it make sense.

Never be afraid to ask the news editor or a senior colleague if you're confused about what you're trying to find out. Better a moment's embarrassment before you start than the humiliation of realising, after you've written your story, that you've been missing the point all along.

The same applies when you're interviewing. Never be afraid to ask apparently obvious questions – if you have to.

The trick, though, is to be well briefed – and then ask your questions. Try to know more than a reporter would be expected to know; but don't parade your knowledge: ask your questions in a straightforward way.

Challenge when necessary, probe certainly, interrupt if you have to – but never argue when you're interviewing. Be polite, firm, controlled, professional. It may sound old-fashioned but you represent your publication and its readers.

'Errors of fact do more to undermine the trust and confidence of readers than any other sin we commit. A story is only as good as the dumbest error in it.'
　　Donald D Jones

Routine is vital to news gathering. Always read your own publication – and its rivals – regularly; maintain your contacts book and diary; remember to ask people their ages if that is what the news editor insists on. Above all, when interviewing, *get people's names right*.

Factual accuracy is vital to credible news journalism. A bright and clever story is worse than useless if its content is untrue: more people will read it – and more people will be misinformed.

NEWS FORMULAS

The two most commonly quoted formulas in the traditional approach to news writing are Rudyard Kipling's six questions (sometimes abbreviated to the five Ws) and the news pyramid (usually described as 'inverted').

The six questions

Kipling's six questions – who, what, how, where, when, why – are a useful checklist for news stories, and it's certainly possible to write an intro that includes them all. The much-quoted textbook example is:

> Lady Godiva (WHO) rode (WHAT) naked (HOW) through the streets of Coventry (WHERE) yesterday (WHEN) in a bid to cut taxes (WHY).

This is facetiously called the clothesline intro – because you can hang everything on it. There is nothing wrong with this particular example but there is no reason why every news intro should be modelled on it. Indeed some intros would become very unwieldy if they tried to answer all six questions.

'I keep six honest serving-men
(They taught me all I knew);
Their names are What and Why and When
And How and Where and Who.'
    Rudyard Kipling

In general, the six questions should all be answered somewhere in the story – but there are exceptions. For example, in a daily paper a reporter may have uncovered a story several days late. They will try to support it with quotes obtained 'yesterday'; but there is no point in emphasising to readers that they are getting the story late. So the exact date on which an event took place should not be given unless it is relevant.

In weekly newspapers and periodicals 'this week' may be relevant; 'last week' as a regular substitute for the daily newspaper's 'yesterday' is usually pointless. Even worse is 'recently', which carries a strong whiff of staleness and amateurism – best left to the club newsletter and the parish magazine.

So the six questions should be kept as a checklist. When you've written a news story, check whether you've failed to answer one of the questions – and so weakened your story. But if there is no point in answering a particular question, don't bother to answer it.

Two of these questions – who and what – are obviously essential. In all news intros somebody or something must do or experience something. A useful distinction can be made between 'who' stories, in which the focus is on the person concerned, and 'what' stories, which are dominated by what happens. As we shall see, drawing this distinction can help you decide whether or not to include a person's name in an intro.

The news pyramid

This particular pyramid is not quite as old as the ancient Egyptians. But as a formula for analysing, teaching and practising news writing it goes back a long way. And the pyramid is certainly a useful idea (the only mystery is why most commentators insist on 'inverting' it – turning it upside down – when it does the job perfectly well the right way up).

The purpose of the pyramid is to show that the points in a news story are made in descending order of importance. News is written so that readers can stop reading when they have satisfied their curiosity – without worrying that something important is being held back. To put it another way, news is written so that sub-editors can cut stories from the bottom up – again, without losing something important.

As we shall see, some stories don't fit the pyramid idea as well as others – but it remains a useful starting point for news writing.

INTROS 1: TRADITIONAL

The news intro should be able to stand on its own. Usually one sentence, it conveys the essence of the story in a clear, concise, punchy way: general enough to be understood; precise enough to be distinguished from other stories.

It should contain few words – usually fewer than 30, often fewer than 20.

First, decide what your story is about: like any other sentence a news intro has a subject. Then ask yourself two questions: why this story now? and how would you start telling your reader the story if you met them in the pub?

The intro is your chance to grab your reader's attention so that they read the story. If you fail, the whole lot goes straight on to the floor of the parrot's cage.

'Too little specific content makes an intro vague; too much is bewildering.'
  Harold Evans

The intro should make sense instantly to your reader. Often it should say how the story will affect them, what it means in practice. And always prefer the concrete to the abstract.

- Don't start with questions or with things that need to be explained – direct quotes, pronouns, abbreviations (except the most common).
- Don't start with things that create typographical problems – figures, italics, direct quotes again.
- Don't start with things that slow the sentence – subordinate clauses, participles, parentheses, long, difficult, foreign words.
- Don't start with when and where, how and why.
- Do start with a crisp sentence in clear English that tells the whole story vividly.

When you've written the whole story, go back and polish your intro; then see if you can use it to write a working news headline. That will tell you whether you've still got more work to do.

Who or what?

If everybody were equal in news terms, all intros might be general and start: 'A man', 'A company', 'A football team'. Alternatively, they might all be specific and start: 'Tony Blair'/'John Evans'; 'ICI'/'Evans Hairdressing'; 'Arsenal'/'Brize Norton Rangers'.

Between 'A man' and 'Tony Blair'/'John Evans' there are various steps: 'An Islington man' is one; 'A New Labour politician'/'An Islington hairdresser' another. Then there's the explaining prefix that works as a title: 'New Labour leader Tony Blair'/'Islington hairdresser John Evans' (though some broadsheets still refuse to use this snappy 'tabloid' device).

'Everyone knows the old saying: if you can't get their attention in the first sentence (or the first eight seconds) they won't bother with the rest.'
Nicholas Bagnall

But the point is that people are not equally interesting in news terms. Some are so well known that their name is enough to sell a story however trivial. Others will only get into the paper by winning the national lottery or dying in a car crash.

Here is a typical WHO intro about a celebrity – without his name there would be no national paper story:

> Comic Eddie Izzard fought back when he was attacked in the street by an abusive drunk, a court heard yesterday.
> *Daily Mail*

Note the contrast with:

> A Crown Court judge who crashed his Range Rover while five times over the drink-drive limit was jailed for five months yesterday.
> *Daily Telegraph*

A Crown Court judge he may be – but not many *Telegraph* readers would recognise his name: it is his occupation not his name that makes this a front-page story.

And finally the anonymous figure 'A man' – his moment of infamy is entirely due to what he has done:

> A man acquitted of murder was convicted yesterday of harassing the family of a police officer who helped investigate him.
> *Guardian*

So the first question to ask yourself in writing an intro is whether your story is essentially WHO or WHAT: is the focus on the person or on what they've done? This helps to answer the question: does the person's name go in the intro or is their identification delayed to the second or third par?

Local papers tend to have stories about 'an Islington man' where the nationals prefer 'a hairdresser' and trade papers go straight to 'top stylist John Evans'. On the sports page both locals and nationals use 'Arsenal' and their nickname 'the Gunners'. In their own local paper Brize Norton Rangers may be 'Rangers'; but when they play Arsenal in the FA Cup, to everybody else they have to become something like 'the non-League club Brize Norton' or 'non-Leaguers Brize Norton'.

When?

There is an exception to the general rule that you shouldn't begin by answering the WHEN question:

> Two years after merchant bank Barings collapsed with £830m losses, it is back in hot water.
> *Daily Mail*

If starting this way gives the story a strong angle, by all means do it. (And the same argument could apply to WHERE, HOW and WHY – but such occasions are rare.)

After

'After' is a useful way of linking two stages of a story without having to say 'because'. Always use 'after' rather than 'following' to do this: it is shorter, clearer – and not journalistic jargon.

> A Cambridge student who killed two friends in a drunken car crash last July yesterday left court a free man after a plea for clemency from one of the victims' parents.
> *Guardian*

In this case the judge may have been influenced by the plea for clemency – but even if he was, that would still not enable the reporter to say 'because'.

> A woman artist was on the run last night after threatening to shoot three judges in the Royal Courts of Justice.
> *Daily Mail*

Here the first part of the intro is an update on the second.

In some stories the 'after' links the problem with its solution:

> A six-year-old boy was rescued by firemen after he became wedged under a portable building being used as a polling station.
> *Daily Telegraph*

In others the 'after' helps to explain the first part of the intro:

> An aboriginal man was yesterday speared 14 times in the legs and beaten on the head with a nulla nulla war club in a traditional punishment after Australia's courts agreed to recognise tribal justice.
> *Guardian*

Sometimes 'after' seems too weak to connect the two parts of an intro:

> Examiners were accused of imposing a 'tax on Classics' yesterday after announcing they would charge sixth formers extra to take A-levels in Latin and Greek.
> *Daily Mail*

It is certainly true that A happened after B – but it also happened because of B. There should be a stronger link between the two parts of the intro.

One point or two?

As far as possible intros should be about one point not two, and certainly not several. The double intro can sometimes work:

> Bill Clinton has completed his selection of the most diverse Cabinet in US history by appointing the country's first woman law chief.
>
> The President-elect also picked a fourth black and a second Hispanic to join his top team.
> *Daily Mail*

Here the *Mail* reporter (or sub) has divided the intro into two separate pars. It's easier to read this way.

> Australian Lucas Parsons equalled the course record with a nine-under-par 64, but still could not quite take the spotlight away from Tiger Woods in the first round of the Australian Masters in Melbourne yesterday.
> *Daily Telegraph*

Yes, it's a bit long but the reporter just gets away with it. Everybody is expecting to read about current hero Tiger Woods but here's this sensation – a course record by a little-known golfer.

In some stories the link between two points is so obvious that a concise double intro is probably the only way to go. In the two examples below 'both' makes the point:

> Battersea's boxing brothers Howard and Gilbert Eastman both maintained their undefeated professional records at the Elephant and Castle Leisure Centre last Saturday.
> Wandsworth Borough *Guardian*

> Loftus Road – owner of Queens Park Rangers – and Sheffield United both announced full-year operating losses.
> *Guardian*

(Obvious or not, the link does give problems in developing the story – see over.)

The main cause of clutter in news stories is trying to say too much in the intro. This makes the intro itself hard to read – and the story hard to develop clearly. Here is a cluttered intro:

> The Chancellor, Gordon Brown, will arrive in Northern Ireland today to announce an investment package of at least £150 million, far in excess of the predicted amount, as the Government increases efforts to secure a Yes vote in the referendum on the Good Friday agreement.
> *Guardian*

As well as making its two main points, connected by 'as', the intro wastes time and space on the incidental fact of Brown's visit and the pompous parenthesis 'far in excess of the predicted amount'. The intro raises rather than answers a question – is the package a bribe to Northern Ireland voters? – which is answered only in the fourth par.

As and when

'As' is often used in intros to link two events that occur at the same time:

> A National Lottery millionaire was planning a lavish rerun of her wedding last night as a former colleague claimed she was being denied her rightful share of the jackpot.
> *Daily Telegraph*

This approach rarely works. Here the main point of the story is not A (the planned second wedding) but B (the dispute) – as is shown by the fact that the next 10 pars develop it; the 11th par covers the wedding plans; and the final four pars return to the dispute.

By contrast with 'as', 'when' is often used for intros that have two bites at the cherry: the first grabs the reader's attention; the second justifies the excitement:

> A crazed woman sparked panic in the High Court yesterday when she burst in and held a gun to a judge's head.
> *Sun*

> A naive Oxford undergraduate earned a double first from the university of life when he was robbed by two women in one day, a court heard today.
> London *Evening Standard*

This is a tabloid technique but none the worse for that.

Specific or summary?

Should an intro begin with an example then generalise – or make a general statement then give an example? Should it be specific – or summary/portmanteau/comprehensive?

> Torrential rain in Spain fell mainly on the lettuces last month – and it sent their prices rocketing.
> *Guardian*

This intro to a story on retail price inflation grabs the attention in a way that a general statement would not. Whenever possible, choose a specific news point rather than a general statement for your intro.

But weather reports can be exceptions. Here's the first par of a winter weather story:

> The first snowfalls of winter brought much of the South East to a standstill today after temperatures plunged below freezing. The wintry onslaught claimed its first victim when a motorist was killed in Kent.
> London *Evening Standard*

Pity about 'plunged' and 'wintry onslaught' – they were probably in the cuttings for last year's snow story too. But otherwise the intro works well for the *Standard*, which covers much of the south east around London. A Kent paper would have led on the death.

The wider the area your paper covers the greater the argument for a general intro on a weather story.

Fact or claim?

This is a vital distinction in news. Are you reporting something as fact – or reporting that somebody has said something in a speech or a written report? An avalanche of news comes by way of reports and surveys; courts, councils and tribunals; public meetings and conferences.

In these stories you must attribute – say who said it – in the intro. Tabloids sometimes delay the attribution to the second or third pars – but this practice is not recommended: it risks confusion in the reader's mind.

> Skiers jetting off for the slopes are risking a danger much worse than broken bones, according to university research published today.
> *Guardian*

Note that this is a general not a detailed attribution – that comes later in the story. Only give a name in the intro when it is likely to be recognised by the reader.

The WHO/WHAT distinction is important in these stories. The rule is to start with what is said – unless the person saying it is well known, as in:

> Pope John Paul II yesterday urged the United States to reconsider its 35-year economic embargo against Cuba.
> *Guardian*

If your story is based on a speech or written report you give the detail (e.g. WHERE) lower in the story. But if it is based on a press conference or routine interview, there is no need to mention this. Writing 'said at a press conference' or 'said in a telephone interview' is like nudging the reader and saying 'I'm a journalist, really'.

Some publications, particularly trade periodicals, are inclined to parade the fact that they have actually interviewed somebody for a particular news story, as in 'told the *Muckshifters' Gazette*'. This is bad style because it suggests that on other occasions no interview has taken place – that the publication's news stories are routinely based on unchecked press releases. Where this is standard practice, it is stretching a point to call it 'news writing'.

Past, present – or future?

Most news intros report what happened, so are written in the past tense. But some are written in the present tense, which is more immediate, more vivid to the reader:

> An advert for Accurist watches featuring an ultra-thin model is being investigated by the Advertising Standards Authority.
> *Guardian*

News of the investigation makes a better intro than the fact that people have complained to the ASA: as well as being more immediate it takes the story a stage further.

Some intros combine the present tense for the latest stage in the story with the past tense for the facts that grab the attention:

> BT is tightening up its telephone security system after its confidential list of ex-directory numbers was penetrated – by a woman from Ruislip.
> *Observer*

This intro also illustrates two other points: the use of AFTER to link two stages of a story (see above) and THE ELEMENT OF SURPRISE (see over). The dash emphasises the point that this huge and powerful organisation was apparently outwitted by a mere individual.

Speech-report intros are often written with the first part in the present tense and the second in the past:

> Copyright is freelances' work and they must never give it away, said Carol Lee, who is coordinating the NUJ campaign against the *Guardian*'s new rights offensive.
> *Journalist*

Note that the first part of the intro is not a quote. Quotes are not used in good news intros for two main reasons: as Harold Evans noted in 1972,

> Offices where intros are still set with drop caps usually ban quote intros because of the typographical complications. There is more against them than that. The reader has to do too much work. He has to find out who is speaking and he may prefer to move on.

The use of the male pronoun has dated – but the rule holds good.

When you write the intro for a speech report, take the speaker's main point and, if necessary, put it in your own words. Thus the version you end up with may or may not be the actual words of the speaker. In this example we don't know what Carol Lee's words were – but they could have been more elaborate.

Here, the editing process could have gone further. A more concise version of the intro would be:

> Freelances must never give up copyright, said Carol Lee . . .

Some present-tense intros look forward to the future:

> Yule Catto, the chemicals group, is believed to be preparing a £250m bid for Holliday Chemical, its sector rival.
> *Sunday Times*

And some intros are actually written in the future tense:

> More than 1,000 travel agency shops will unite this week to become the UK's largest High Street package holiday chain, using the new name WorldChoice.
> *Observer*

Where possible, use the present or the future tense rather than the past and, if you're making a prediction, be as definite as you can safely be.

The element of surprise

> A woman who fell ill with a collapsed lung on a Boeing 747 had her life saved by two doctors who carried out an operation with a coathanger, a bottle of mineral water, brandy and a knife and fork.
> *Guardian*

> Two British doctors carried out a life-saving operation aboard a jumbo jet – with a coat hanger.
> *Daily Mail*

> A doctor saved a mum's life in a mid-air operation – using a coathanger, pen top, brandy and half a plastic bottle.
> *Sun*

These three intros agree with one another more than they disagree: a woman's life was saved in mid-air by doctors using what lay to hand including a coathanger.

The best way of writing the intro puts the human drama first but does not leave the intriguing aspect of the means used until later in the story. That would risk the reader saying 'Good but so what?' – and going on to something else.

Nor in this kind of story should you begin with the bizarre. 'A coathanger, pen top, brandy and half a plastic bottle were used in an emergency mid-air operation . . . ' misplaces the emphasis. In any newspaper the fact that a woman's life was saved comes first.

'Clarity, tightness, information – and the news point that is going to start people talking. These are the qualities to seek.'
   Leslie Sellers on news intros

In the three intros quoted above there are various strengths and weaknesses: the *Guardian* is longwinded and clumsy, though accurate and informative; the *Mail* is concise, but is 'a jumbo jet' better than 'a Boeing 747' (in the intro who cares what make of plane it was?) and why just a coathanger – what happened to the brandy? The *Sun* spares us the planespotter details but insists on calling the woman 'a mum' (while failing to mention her children anywhere in the story).

And is the story mainly about a woman (*Guardian*), a doctor (*Sun*) or two British doctors (*Mail*)?

But in style the biggest contrast here is between the approach of the *Mail* and the *Sun* which both signal the move from human drama to bizarre detail by using the dash – and that of the *Guardian* which does not.

When you start with an important fact, then want to stress an unusual or surprising aspect of the story in the same sentence, the natural way to do this is with the dash. It corresponds exactly with the way you would pause and change your tone of voice in telling the story.

The running story

When a story runs from day to day it would irritate the reader to keep talking about 'A man' in the intro. Also it would be pointless: most readers either read the paper regularly or follow the news in some other way. But it is essential that each news story as a whole should include necessary background for new readers.

> The tiger which bit a circus worker's arm off was the star of the famous Esso TV commercial.
> London *Evening Standard*

After this intro the story gives an update on the victim's condition and repeats details of the accident.

Court reports are often running stories. Here the trick is to write an intro that works for both sets of readers: it should be both vivid and informative.

> The 10-year-old girl alleged to have been raped by classmates in a primary school toilet said yesterday that she just wanted to be a 'normal kid'.
> *Guardian*

In some cases phrases like 'renewed calls' or 'a second death' make the point that this is one more stage in a continuing drama:

> Another Catholic man was shot dead in Belfast last night just as
> the IRA issued a warning that the peace process in Northern
> Ireland was on borrowed time.
> *Guardian*

The follow-up

Like the running story, the follow-up should not start 'A man' if the
original story is likely to be remembered. In the following example
the 'mystery businessman' has enjoyed a second expensive meal weeks
after the first – but the story is his identity. His name is given in par three.

> The mystery businessman who spent more than £13,000 on a
> dinner for three in London is a 34-year-old Czech financier who
> manages a £300m fortune.
> *Sunday Times*

INTROS 2: VARIATION

The possible variations are endless: any feature-writing technique can be
applied to news writing – if it works. But two variations are particularly
common: selling the story and the narrative style. The narrative
sometimes turns into the delayed drop.

Selling the story

Here a selling intro is put in front of a straight news story:

> If you have friends or relations in High Street banking, tell them
> – warn them – to find another job. Within five years, the Internet
> is going to turn their world upside down.
>
> This is the confident forecast in a 200-page report . . .
> *Daily Mail*

The report's forecast is that the Internet will turn the world of banking
upside down – that is where the straight news story starts. But the *Mail*
reporter has added an intro that dramatises the story and says what it will
mean in practice – for people like the reader.

> They were the jeans that launched (or relaunched) a dozen pop
> songs.

> Now Levis, the clothing manufacturer that used to turn everything it touched into gold, or even platinum, has fallen on harder times.
>
> Yesterday the company announced that it is to cut its North American workforce by a third.
> *Guardian*

The straight news in par three follows an intro that gives the story a nostalgic flavour: the reader is brought into the story and reminded of their pleasurable past buying jeans and listening to pop music.

The risk with this kind of selling intro is that some readers may be turned off by it: they may not have friends in retail banking; they may not feel nostalgic about jeans and pop music. What is important here is knowing your readers and how they are likely to react.

The narrative style

Here the traditional news story approach gives way to the kind of narrative technique used in fiction:

> The thud of something falling to the ground stopped Paul Hallett in his tracks as he tore apart the rafters of an old outside lavatory.
>
> The handyman brushed off his hands and picked up a dusty wallet, half expecting to find nothing inside.
>
> But picking through the contents one by one, Mr Hallett realised he had stumbled upon the details of a US Air Force chaplain stationed at a nearby RAF base in Suffolk 50 years earlier.
> *Daily Mail*

> Choral scholar Gavin Rogers-Ball was dying for a cigarette. Stuck on a coach bringing the Wells Cathedral choir back from a performance in Germany, he had an idea – ask one of the boys to be sick and the adult members of the choir could step off the bus for a smoke.
>
> It was a ruse that was to cost the alto dear . . .
> *Guardian*

Both stories begin with a dramatic moment – and name their main character. As with fiction the trick is to get the reader involved with that person and what happens to them.

News stories about court cases and tribunals can often be handled in this way, and so can any light or humorous subject. But for the technique to work there must be a story worth telling.

If you can, try to avoid the awkward use of variation words to describe your main character. 'Alto' in the *Guardian* story is particularly clumsy (See 'Variation' on pages 39–40.)

The delayed drop

Here the intro is in narrative style but the story soon changes direction. The change is usually signalled by a 'but':

> A pint-sized Dirty Harry, aged 11, terrorised a school when he pulled out a Magnum revolver in the playground. Screaming children fled in panic as the boy, who could hardly hold the powerful handgun, pointed it at a teacher.
>
> But headmaster Arthur Casson grabbed the boy and discovered that the gun – made famous by Clint Eastwood in the film Dirty Harry – was only a replica.
> *Daily Mirror*

> A naughty nurse called Janet promised kinky nights of magic to a married man who wrote her passionate love letters.
>
> He was teased with sexy photographs, steamy suggestions and an offer to meet her at a hotel.
>
> But soon he was being blackmailed . . . the girl of his dreams was really a man called Brian.
> *Daily Mirror*

In terms of entertainment a well-told delayed-drop story is hard to beat.

STRUCTURE

News is all about answering questions – the reader's. The best guide to developing a news story is to keep asking yourself: what does the reader need or want to know now?

1 Building the pyramid

First the intro must be amplified, extended, explained, justified. For example, in a WHAT story where the main character is not named in the intro, the reader needs to know something more about them: certainly their name, probably their age and occupation, perhaps other details depending on the story. A CLAIM story where the intro gives only a general attribution – 'according to a survey' – needs a detailed attribution later on.

These are obvious, routine and in a sense formal points – similarly, a sport story needs the score, a court story details of the charges, and so on.

A common development of a news intro in the classic news pyramid is to take the story it contains and retell it in greater detail:

Intro

A six-year-old boy was rescued by firemen after he became wedged under a portable building being used as a polling station.

Retelling of intro

Jack Moore was playing with friends near his home in Nevilles Cross Road, Hebburn, South Tyneside, when curiosity got the better of him and he crawled into the eight-inch space under the building, where he became firmly wedged.

Firemen used airbags to raise the cabin before Jack was freed . . .

Further information and quote

. . . and taken to hospital, where he was treated for cuts and bruising and allowed home. His mother, Lisa, said: 'He is a little shaken and bruised but apart from that he seems all right.'
Daily Telegraph

In a longer story the intro can be retold twice, each time with more detail:

Intro

A woman artist was on the run last night after threatening to shoot three judges in the Royal Courts of Justice.

First retelling of intro

Annarita Muraglia, who is in her early 20s, stood up in the public gallery brandishing what appeared to be a Luger and ran towards the judges screaming: 'If anybody moves I am going to shoot.'

Two judges tried to reason with her as the third calmly left court 7 to raise the alarm.

Within minutes armed response units and police dog handlers surrounded the huge Victorian gothic building.

But Muraglia, who has twice been jailed for contempt in the past – for stripping in court and throwing paint at a judge – disappeared into the warren of corridors.

The drama brought chaos to central London for five hours as roads around the Strand were closed. As hundreds of court staff were evacuated an RAF helicopter was drafted in to help 80 police on the ground.

Second retelling of intro

Witnesses said Lord Justice Beldam, 71, Mrs Justice Bracewell, 62, and Mr Justice Mance, 54, were hearing a routine criminal appeal when Muraglia – who had no connection with the case – stood up in the gallery.

'She was holding a gun American-style with both hands and seemed deranged,' said barrister Tom MacKinnon. 'She told the judges: "I demand you hear my case right now or I will start shooting."

'Mrs Justice Bracewell tried to reason with her but the woman started waving the gun, threatening to shoot anybody who moved.'

Lord Justice Beldam, one of the most senior High Court judges, calmly urged her to put down her gun as members of the public and lawyers sat in stunned silence.

Senior court registrar Roy Armstrong bravely approached her and asked for details of her case, but she then fled through a door to the judges' chambers.

Further information: background

Italy-born Muraglia, from Islington, North London, was jailed for contempt in December 1994 after breaking furniture and attacking staff at a child custody hearing.

Later, during a review of her sentence, she dropped her trousers to reveal her bare bottom painted with the words 'Happy Christmas'.

In July 1995, she sprayed green paint over the wig of Judge Andrew Brooks. The following month when he sentenced her to 15 months for contempt she again bared her bottom and was escorted away screaming: 'So you don't want to see my bottom again, Wiggy?'

Further information: update

> Police said last night that they did not know if the gun was real or
> fake. They were confident of making an arrest.
> *Daily Mail*

Alternatively, the intro may be followed by information on events
leading up to it before the intro is restated:

Intro

> Comic Eddie Izzard fought back when he was attacked in the street
> by an abusive drunk, a court heard yesterday.

Events leading up to intro

> The award-winning comedian, who wears skirts and make-up
> on stage, had been taunted by jobless Matthew Dodkin after a
> stand-up show at the Corn Exchange, Cambridge, last November.
> Magistrates in the city heard that 22-year-old Dodkin had put his
> hands on his waist while running his tongue round his lips and
> saying: 'Ooh, Tracy.'
>
> Mr Izzard admitted: 'I was very abusive towards him and I said he
> deserved to be cut with a knife.' . . .

Retelling of intro

> . . . Dodkin then attacked him. 'I punched back and I struck
> blows, which is surprising because the last fight I had I was 12,'
> said Mr Izzard, 35, who suffered a cut lip and a black eye.

Further information

> Dodkin, of Queensway Flats, Cambridge, declined to give evidence
> after denying common assault. He was fined £120 and ordered to
> pay £100 compensation.
> *Daily Mail*

The intro may be followed by explanation – of a single aspect of the intro
or of the intro as a whole:

Intro

> An advert for Accurist watches featuring an ultra-thin model is
> being investigated by the Advertising Standards Authority.

Explanation of intro

The woman has a silver watch wrapped round her upper arm, with the slogan: 'Put some weight on.'

'We're investigating it on the grounds that it might be distressing and upsetting to people with eating disorders,' said a spokesman for the authority. It had received 78 complaints from people with anorexia or bulimia, from relatives and friends of sufferers, and from the Eating Disorder Association.

Further information and quotes

An Accurist spokesman said the company had also received complaints, and claimed that the advertisement was no longer running. 'There was never any intention to cause distress,' he said.

Models One, the agency used by Zoya, the model in question, said that she was naturally thin and 'an exceptionally beautiful girl'.
Guardian

Quotes from the people and organisations involved in stories are an essential part of their development. The story above, having quoted the Advertising Standards Authority, includes comments from the company and model agency. Readers – except the most bigoted – want to be given both sides of a story.

Conflicts between people and organisations – in politics, business, court cases – often make news. If the issue is complicated, the intro should be an attempt to simplify it without distortion. As the story is developed it will become easier to deal with the complications.

In the story below the reporter (or sub) has decided to lead on the technical victory won by McDonald's and not overload the intro by including the fact that two of the claims made by the Green campaigners were found to be justified. But this fact must be included early in the story.

Intro

McDonald's won a hollow victory over two Green campaigners yesterday after the longest libel trial in history.

First retelling of intro

The hamburger corporation was awarded £60,000 damages over a leaflet which savaged its reputation, accusing it of putting profits before people, animal welfare and rain forests.

But the verdict cost more than £10 million in legal bills, which McDonald's will never recover from the penniless protesters who fought for three years in the High Court.

New fact

David Morris and Helen Steel were also claiming victory last night after the judge backed two of their claims. In an 800-page judgment which took six months to prepare, Mr Justice Bell ruled that the company is cruel to animals and that its advertising takes advantage of susceptible young children.

First retelling of intro (continued)

Mr Morris, 43, and 31-year-old Miss Steel are refusing to pay a penny of the damages. 'They don't deserve any money,' said Miss Steel, a part-time barmaid. 'And in any case, we haven't got any.'

Further information – background

The trial began in June 1994 and spanned 314 days in court, involving 180 witnesses and 40,000 pages of documents.

At its heart was the leaflet What's Wrong with McDonald's?, produced by the tiny pressure group London Greenpeace, which is not connected to Greenpeace International. The defendants helped to distribute it in the 1980s.

McDonald's had issued similar libel writs many times before, and opponents had always backed down. But Mr Morris and Miss Steel, vegetarian anarchists from Tottenham, North London, were determined to fight.

The burger firm hired one of the most brilliant legal teams money can buy, headed by Richard Rampton QC. The defendants were forced to represent themselves because there is no legal aid for libel cases.

Former postman Mr Morris, a single parent with an eight-year-old son, appeared in court in casual dress, usually unshaven. Miss Steel, the daughter of a retired company director from Farnham, Surrey, prepared for the case each morning while hanging from a strap on the Piccadilly Line tube.

Second retelling of intro

Yesterday Mr Justice Bell ruled that they had libelled McDonald's by alleging that the corporation ripped down rain forests, contributed to Third World starvation, created excessive waste and sold food which was closely linked with heart disease and cancer.

He said it was also libellous to claim that McDonald's was interested in recruiting only cheap labour and exploited disadvantaged
groups, particularly women and black people, although the claim
was 'partly justified' because the firm pays low wages.

Further information and quotes

The judge also condemned as 'most unfair' the practice of sending
young staff home early if the restaurant was quiet and not paying
them for the rest of their shift.

Critics of the company will also seize on his ruling that McDonald's
'are culpably responsible for cruel practices in the rearing and
slaughter of some of the animals which are used to produce their
food'.

After the hearing, McDonald's UK president Paul Preston said he
had no wish to bankrupt Mr Morris and Miss Steel. 'This was not a
matter of costs, it was a matter of truth,' he said.

But the case has been a public relations disaster for McDonald's,
cast in the role of a hugely rich corporation using its financial
muscle to suppress debate on important issues. Far from
the leaflet being suppressed, two million copies have now been
handed out around the world.
Daily Mail

2 Splitting the pyramid

The pyramid structure is far easier to sustain if the intro is single rather
than double. One of the problems with A + B intros is that they are
difficult to develop coherently. The double intro below illustrates the
problem:

Intro (A)

Bill Clinton has completed his selection of the most diverse Cabinet
in US history by appointing the country's first woman law chief.

Intro (B)

The President-elect also picked a fourth black and a second
Hispanic to join his top team.

Retelling of intro A

Zoe Baird, currently general counsel for the insurance company
Aetna Life & Casualty, will be his Attorney General.

Retelling of intro B

> Black representative Mike Espy was named Mr Clinton's secretary for agriculture while former mayor of Denver Federico Pena, a Hispanic, will be responsible for transport issues.
> *Daily Mail*

Another strategy for the double intro is to develop part A before returning to part B:

Intro (A + B)

> Australian Lucas Parsons equalled the course record with a nine-under-par 64, but still could not quite take the spotlight away from Tiger Woods in the first round of the Australian Masters in Melbourne yesterday.

Retelling of intro A

> Parsons fired six birdies on the front nine before holing his second shot at the par four 13th for an eagle two – the highlight of the round. His approach shot landed on the green and bounced two metres beyond the flag, but then spun back into the hole.
>
> Parsons now shares the Huntingdale course record with compatriot Mike Clayton and German Bernhard Langer.

Quotes supporting intro A

> 'My game has been getting better over recent months. This is a course I know and I can play well here,' said Parsons.
>
> 'I got off to a good start today and it just kept happening. I just went with the flow.'

Retelling of intro B

> But Woods, who won the Bangkok Classic in Thailand on Sunday, his fourth tournament victory since turning professional last August, was still the centre of attention.

Development of B and quotes

> He also enjoyed the long holes to finish at five-under-par 68 for a share of fifth place to remain in contention.
>
> The 21-year-old big-hitting American birdied all four par fives on the par-73 course to the delight of a large gallery, even though he only used his driver once.

'I grinded my way around there and came in with a good score. Off the tee, it was probably one of my better ball-striking rounds in a while,' Woods said.

'It was just the mental grind of playing a golf course that requires accuracy and so much precision off the tee. You don't really have a chance to relax.

'I haven't played my best golf today. I just made one birdie besides the par fives and that's not saying a whole lot.'

Further information

Australian Peter O'Malley held second place with a 65. Former US Masters champion Larry Mize finished on five-under along-side Woods, while defending champion Craig Parry, of Australia, struggled to a 73.
Daily Telegraph

Splitting the pyramid always presents problems. Either, as in the first example above, you make the reader hop about from A to B as the story unfolds – now it's A, now it's B. Or, as in the second example, you develop A fully before turning to B. The problem here is that B can get forgotten before the reader gets there.

It cannot be stressed too strongly that the best intro is always the simplest: try to find one point for your intro rather than two – or more.

In terms of development this may mean (as in the *Daily Mail* story on McDonald's above) that you need to introduce important material not covered by the intro early in the story. But that is a better solution than cluttering the intro and confusing the general development of the story.

3 Exceptions to the pyramid

Don't worship the pyramid: it is only a way of visualising the most common structure of a traditional news story. The guiding principle in developing a news story is: what does the reader need or want to know now? If answering their questions means abandoning the pyramid, so be it.

Speech reports, for example, are not necessarily written in strict pyramid form. They should start with the most important point made by the speaker – but this will often be followed by other points that have little to do with the first. Of course, you should try to put these secondary points in order of importance but this may seem a pretty arbitrary process.

However, to keep the pyramid idea, each point can be seen as a mini-pyramid with its own intro, development and elaborating quote; thus the story can become a series of small pyramids.

4 The narrative style

The clearest example of non-pyramid news writing is a story in the narrative style, which begins with a dramatic moment and carries on to the end – often the point of the story. If you cut a narrative news story from the end you destroy it.

The one concession made to conventional news writing is that the main character is often asked for a quote, which is added on after the narrative ending.

Intro

> When Bernard Warner examined the lobster it did not strike him as being particularly odd. The crustacean looked paler than its rivals but it had arrived at Mr Warner's fishmonger shop in Doncaster as part of a routine delivery from the East coast, so there could not be anything unusual about it, could there?

Story continues

> Deciding the animal was simply suffering from old age, Mr Warner flew to Madeira on holiday. En route, his in-flight magazine fell open at an article about albino lobsters.

> A white lobster caught off the American coast was sold for £15,000, the article told him. A bigger version caught off Filey was insured for £20,000.

Story ends

> Mr Warner raced to a phone after touching down. 'Don't sell that lobster,' he breathlessly told his family firm. It was too late. The creature – worth £20,000 – had been sold on at the normal market rate, boiled and digested by an unsuspecting diner somewhere.

Quote

> Mr Warner, who has been in the fish business for 40 years, sells his lobsters to restaurants and private customers throughout the country, and he has no idea where his prize catch went.

He said: 'I couldn't believe it. In all my time as a fishmonger I've never come across one before. I'm pig sick.'

'Someone has had a very valuable meal without even knowing it. For me it's like winning the lottery and then discovering you have thrown the ticket away.'
Guardian

NEWS STYLE

News style is – or ought to be – plain, simple, clear, so that the story tells itself. For a detailed discussion of this issue, see the final chapter.

Variation

One of the worst news-writing habits you can acquire is to avoid calling a spade a spade – or rather, having called it a spade in the intro, to insist on calling it a gardening tool, a digging device and then a horticultural implement in the pars that follow.

'In news writing the most effective prose style is one that is imperceptible to most of the readers.'
James Aitchison

This practice is based on two false assumptions: one, that the repetition of words like spade is always a bad idea; two, that attentive readers enjoy these variation words for their own sake.

Precisely the opposite is true – as is shown by the story above. A lively tale about a special kind of lobster is weakened by the inept use of a series of variation words to refer to it: 'crustacean' in par one; 'animal' in par two; 'creature' in par four.

These words add nothing: they are clearly examples of variation for its own sake. And if the reader has half an ear they grate. 'Crustacean' is particularly naff: it echoes those old football reports where 'the 35-year-old goalkeeper Wally Jones' becomes 'the veteran net-minder' in the next par.

By contrast the reporter just gets away with 'prize catch' in par five – though it would have been better if Mr Warner had done the catching in the first place. But it was a prize; it had been caught; and the phrase adds the right kind of emphasis.

This kind of variation has traditionally been called 'elegant' – because it's intended to embellish, to add colour to copy. In general, it's an example of how not to write.

Then there is variation to avoid unintended repetition. Your ear should tell you when this is necessary. But remember that the plainer the word the less noticeable it is when repeated, so don't bother to avoid repeating words like 'said' and 'says'.

Sometimes repetition tells you that the sentence itself is badly constructed – too long, too loose, too complicated. Here's an example with the repeated word in italic type:

> A mother of three young *children*, jailed for two months after lying about a traffic accident, was yesterday reunited with her *children* after she was freed by three Appeal Court judges – but they reiterated the gravity of the offence and said the plight of her *children* had tipped the balance in favour of her release.
> *Guardian*

About the only thing to be said in favour of this intro is that 'children' does not become 'offspring' in the second case and 'progeny' or 'issue' in the third. If you find yourself writing a sentence like this, don't struggle to replace the repeated words: rewrite the sentence altogether in a simpler way.

Quotes

First, in general, use said/says to introduce and attribute quotes, though told/tells is a useful variation, as in 'the minister told MPs'. So do not write:

> 'Speaking at the meeting the speaker said'

but:

> 'The speaker told the meeting'.

Always avoid variations like 'claim', 'admit', 'state', 'remark', 'point out', 'explain', 'refute' – unless you intend the precise meaning conveyed by the word.

Do not use 'he added' because you think the quote has been going on long enough and are too lazy to think up some other way of getting to the next bit. Keep 'he added' for cases where there is a pause, an afterthought or a contrast as in:

> He said it would probably rain – but he added: 'We need it.'

Where possible use the present tense – 'says' – instead of the past – 'said'.

When somebody is quoted for the first time put the attribution at the beginning, as in:

> John Smith says: 'I'm furious.'

If the attribution does not come at the beginning, put it after the first complete sentence – not in the middle of it and not at the end of the complete quote. This is the way to do it:

> 'I'm furious,' John Smith says. 'I've never been so angry.'

Consistency

Be consistent. Don't change your tone in the middle of a story. Either write in the traditional style or use one of the variations; be serious or light – not both at the same time.

Particularly avoid the facetious remark dropped into a straightforward story.

'The interpolation of a weak joke into a serious news story is so inappropriate that it can only be described as oafish.'
    Keith Waterhouse

Bridges and links

In general news does not need bridges to connect one par with the next. Transitional words and phrases like 'also' – or the pompous equivalent 'in addition' – are rarely necessary. When you start a new sentence or a new par you are effectively saying to the reader: 'also'. That does not mean that these words and phrases are always wrong but you should not strain to include them in traditional news stories.

Journalese and jargon

Most of what is called journalese – whether tabloid ('axe' for 'sack') or broadsheet ('sustain injury' for 'be hurt') – is bad writing and you should avoid it. 'Following' for 'after' is certainly an example of this.

But certain code words can be useful – to maximise the amount of information you can convey to the reader. For example, if you're pretty confident – but not certain – that A will happen, you can write: 'A is set to happen.' You should always try to find out precisely what somebody's role is in something – but if you can't, it's usually better to write 'B is involved with the project' rather than nothing at all.

The same advice covers phrases like 'industry sources say' when your contacts will not give you identified quotes. Inform your reader – but keep the jargon under control.

Names and titles

The convention in journalism is full name ('John/Joan Smith') for the first use, then either courtesy title ('Mr/Mrs/Miss/Ms Smith) or surname or first name for the rest of the story. (For more on this and similar points see the chapter on house style in *English for Journalists*.) Remember, be consistent: never follow 'John Smith' by 'Mr Smith' then 'John'. Again, variation for its own sake irritates the reader.

Endings

In general traditional news stories (as opposed to those in the narrative style) do not have endings – that is, they end where the writer runs out of steam, the sub runs out of space, the reader runs out of interest. But there is no reason why a news story should not end neatly. The exception proves that the rule is one of pragmatism not principle:

> BT is tightening up its telephone security system after its confidential list of ex-directory numbers was penetrated – by a woman from Ruislip.
>
> Working from home, Rachel Barry, a middle-aged married mother, conned BT into revealing the ex-directory numbers of celebrities, sports stars and people in the news . . .

Last week Mrs Barry was convicted by Harrow magistrates of 12 offences of obtaining personal data and selling it to national newspapers . . .

It is believed Mrs Barry had been operating the scam for several years and had earned thousands of pounds. She pleaded guilty to all 12 offences and was fined a total of £1,200 and ordered to pay costs of £800.

Last night the *Observer* was unable to contact Mrs Barry by telephone. She is ex-directory.
Observer

That is an ending.

TWO NEWS STORIES

MAN KILLED AS L-DRIVE CAR PLUNGES OFF CLIFF

A man was feared dead last night after his car ran off a 150ft clifftop into rough seas when his girlfriend lost control while he was giving her a driving lesson.

The woman, in her early 20s, scrambled from the Ford Fiesta as it crashed through a low stone wall at the edge of a car park at the Beacon, St Agnes, on the north Cornwall coast.

Andrew Dunklin, 25, from St Agnes, was trapped in the vehicle as it rolled over the cliff. It is thought he was thrown through the windscreen into the sea. The car came to rest in 30ft of water and immediately began to break up.

The woman raised the alarm and coastguards launched a rescue operation which at its height involved a Navy helicopter, divers, two lifeboats and a cliff rescue team.

Insp Paul Whetter of Devon & Cornwall police said the woman had managed to get out just before the car went over the cliff.

She was treated for shock at the scene by paramedics before being taken to Treliske Hospital in Truro.

A neighbour looking after the missing man's mother at her home in the village said: 'She has just lost her only son.'

The search operation was hampered by worsening weather and a Navy diver had to be pulled out of the sea. The St Agnes and St Ives inshore lifeboats could not get close to the spot.

'We sent our cliff man down to a point about 60ft above the waves, where the cliff became a sheer drop,' said Mike North, sector manager with HM Coastguard. 'He was able to keep an eye on the scene and spotted a lot of debris from the car.

'He saw some clothing and the inshore lifeboat was able to pick up the girl's bag floating in the water.'

A spokesman for RNAS Culdrose added: 'The first diver in the water said it was too dangerous for others to go in. He was being pounded by pieces of wreckage from the car which was being smashed on to the rocks at the bottom of the cliffs.'

The search was called off at 5pm because the situation had become 'too dangerous' for rescue workers. It was to be resumed at first light today.

Mr Dunklin is understood to have been giving his girlfriend a driving lesson on Beacon Road, a remote and little-used track near the cliffs. They may have driven into the gravel-surfaced car park to practise reversing or three-point turns.
Sean O'Neill, *Daily Telegraph*, 7 January 1998

This is a stark and terrible story simply told. The reporter has no need to strain for effect here.

The intro is a bit long at 31 words – a tabloid would have shortened 'when his girlfriend lost control while he was giving her a driving lesson' to something like 'when a driving lesson went wrong'. But because the words and clauses are straightforward, the intro works well enough.

Then, because the intro tells so much of the story, the second par can add dramatic detail as well as locating the story. But do we really want to know what make of car it was? Well, yes, the ordinariness of the Ford Fiesta helps to make this a story about any young couple.

The third par retells the intro; the fourth introduces the rescue operation; but rather than turn the story sideways to cover the search, the reporter rightly concentrates on the two people involved in the accident – and the man's mother.

When we get to it, halfway through the story, the search is described with the aid of powerful quotes. Finally, there's a par on how the couple came to be at the clifftop.

A few quibbles: 'vehicle' in the third par is unnecessary variation for 'car': it follows 'Ford Fiesta'; RNAS (towards the end) should be given in full; in the same par 'added' is particularly strange here, suggesting that the two people quoted were in the same room – and the woman would surely be named if police had released her name.

But in general the reporter has made good use of an opportunity to let a strong story tell itself without clutter and melodramatic language.

HOBBIES PUT JUDGE ON THE ROAD TO RUIN

A judge's entry in Who's Who listed his passions as cars and drinking with friends. Yesterday these twin interests landed John Aspinall QC in court, where he was banned from the road for two and a half years for drink-driving.

Aspinall, 50, who worked as a lorry driver before becoming a lawyer, was more than three times over the limit when he caused a crash on Good Friday.

In Who's Who he lists his recreations as 'motor sports' and 'being with my wife and friends at the Drax Arms' – the country pub near his home in Spetisbury, Dorest, where he is a popular regular.

Now his career is in tatters. He has resigned as a crown court recorder, a part-time judge, and faces a Bar Council disciplinary hearing which could mean being suspended from practising as a barrister or even thrown out of the profession.

He has also resigned from the judicial committee of the governing body of the RAC motorsports council.

Magistrates at Blandford in Dorset were told Aspinall had a blood alcohol level of 122mg. The legal limit is 35mg. He admitted drink-driving and was fined £1,800 and told his ban could be cut by six months if he takes a driver-rehabilitation course.
Daily Mail, 21 May 1998

A routine 'judge banned for drink driving' court report has been turned into a lively story because somebody has bothered to check Aspinall's entry in *Who's Who*.

The all-important intro is a form of delayed drop: the first sentence sets up the second. Then after some basic information on the offence, the sequence is repeated: quotes from *Who's Who* are followed by more on Aspinall's ruined career.

Only in the last par do we get the details of the offence and the magistrates' decision. This must appear somewhere in the story – but only as a tailpiece.

There are blemishes: 'twin interests' in the second sentence is a curious variation on 'passions' in the first; and there is a clumsy phrase in the fourth par, 'which could mean being suspended . . .'

But, as a whole, the story is an example of modern news writing, which grabs the reader's attention, then keeps it by answering their questions.

3
Writing features
Sally Adams

The joy of feature writing lies in its variety. Anything from an agony column to a profile, a product round-up to an obit, can be considered a feature and this variety demands versatility. If there's one word that sums up what good feature writers have it's savvy – not a term found in the news writing chapter, and that tells you a lot.

The sole constraint for features is to write in the way that's right for the publication and its readers. What suits *Car* won't necessarily do for *Custom Car*. What suits *Shoot* is unlikely to work for *Four Four Two* or *When Saturday Comes*. Being so varied, features are hard to define. The safest guide is negative: they're not news.

Not being news they're liberated from spare, functional prose. In place of the breathless messenger they can be entertaining gossips, perceptive analysts, eccentric experts, sympathetic counsellors, bitchy snoops, inspiring guides.

Because they're so varied they're harder to write. They build on everything learnt as a news reporter and in addition demand that writers attract and hold the reader's attention without the benefit of any narrative pull. They can require that writers research and master complicated subjects, then turn huge chunks of information into accessible and digestible form. Reporters rarely mutate effortlessly into feature writers. The apprentice time varies from months to years.

There are guidelines but no absolute rules to rely on for security. Good feature writers take risks; they're the sky divers of print journalism. As 24-hour radio and TV get the news into people's homes first, papers grow more feature-oriented and closer to magazines, and feature writing becomes an ever more important craft.

The guidelines are pretty basic:

- Think
- Focus
- Have something to say
- Take the reader with you from A to Z
- Choose your words carefully and make them flow.

Another difference. Features have extras – and you've just passed the first bullet points/blobs of the chapter, with more to follow.

In ascending order of difficulty, features can inform, help, entertain, persuade and amuse. Gradations exist within all these categories. 'Inform', for example, ranges in difficulty from providing coherent and accessible data to offering analysis and promoting understanding. 'Persuade' ranges in difficulty from prompting a reader to try a new hairstyle to convincing them to try a new lifestyle. Writers achieve these aims by using words their readers feel happy with.

A study of what features editors look for, conducted over many years, produced remarkably consistent answers. The highest common factors were that features should:

- be readable
- be credible
- have a grabbing intro
- involve the reader
- meet the brief
- be accurate
- be crafted
- have substance
- contain an added element of surprise.

Less frequent requirements reflected the varying character of the differing publications:

- table banging
- sparkle
- not jumping around
- sexy
- absorbing
- authoritative

- enthusiastic
- good quotes
- topical
- vigorous
- colourful
- helpful.

Features divide into four main categories:

1   Profiles
    (a) Of individual people, usually based on interviews, which can be:
        written in the first person, ghosted or reported (third person)
        edited down from a tape into Q&As
        in reply to set questions (questionnaire).

        If the subject is dead, these become obits (written by acquaint-
        ance, admirer, enemy, or cobbled together from clippings).

    (b) Of two or more people, or groups; again these can be from
        interviews, or clippings-assisted.

        Subjects can be companies, pop groups, sports teams, orchestras,
        university departments, clubs, councils . . .

2   Product stories: about one product/round-up of many, described,
    compared, tested.

3   Background features, which put news in context.

    'News features' are hybrids, somewhere between a straightforward
    news story and a feature.

    'Colour' pieces describe events as they happen; particularly used for
    funerals and sporting events.

4   Opinion pieces:

    leaders/editorials
    think pieces
    columns
    diaries.

Except in the most staid publications, features have add-ons such as stat
tables, boxes, bullet points and illustrated panels – 'extras' now creeping
on to news pages.

RATING IMPACT

What Philip Larkin, a former chairman of the Booker Prize panel, wrote about assessing a book works just as well for a feature.

> Personally, I found myself asking four questions . . . Could I read it? If I could read it, did I believe it? If I believed it, did I care about it? If I cared, what was the quality of my caring, and would it last?
>
> Few, very few, survived as far as question four. Far too many relied on the classic formula of a beginning, a muddle and an end.

Applying these questions to a feature means asking:

1   Did I read to the end?
2   Was I convinced by what I read?
3   Do I care? Am I going to keep the feature for reference?
4   Am I going to do anything about it? Buy those shoes? Treat employees differently? Change my mind about . . . ?

The important thing about feature writing is pitching the tone of voice and choice of words to the readers. This means that style matters but savvy matters more. So use your wits. Think. Make what you write accessible, interesting, lively, colourful, grabbing, relevant. It's a skill worth acquiring.

A QUICK WORD BEFORE YOU START

The quality of the questions you ask yourself before you start writing is crucial. The sharper your questions, the more likely you are to produce stylish copy. Best advice early on is to think, think again and go on thinking if you're to produce writing that is fresh, appealing and original.

Readers approach features very much as they approach food. Some want simple grub, some fancy cooking, some heavy stodge. Very few relish stale cheese sandwiches or froth. To labour the simile, good ingredients and preparation are essential.

Writing for the reader is the key. This doesn't mean playing safe, always giving them more of what they liked last time. Slavishly following market research has been the death of many a publication. As in showbusiness, what works best is to offer an amalgam of known success and some element of surprise. Features editors, asked to list their requirements, usually include 'something unexpected'.

So, first essential: know your publication and your readers. Wise editors insist that writers should understand the publication's editorial policy. If you don't know what you're trying to do, you're dangerously directionless.

Editorial policies are usually in the infinitive: *to entertain . . . to inform . . . to inspire . . . to persuade.* They then define the readers: *the people of Ludlow and the surrounding district . . . finance directors and budget-holding middle managers in the worldwide telecommunications industry . . . UK university students with an interest in cheap travel outside Europe.*

The last part of the policy usually sets a target: *to be first with the most comprehensive news of the area, building community awareness . . . to help them save money and increase profits through informed analysis of world-wide products/buyers' experiences . . . to provide entertaining, reliable value-for-money reports on the less publicised countries of the developing world.*

To reach people, you should be able to talk their language. It helps to know the following about the readers of your publication:

- how many buy it (circulation)
- how many read it (readership)
- average age range
- male/female split
- years of education – affects vocabulary and sentence complexity
- interests (consumer press)
- job title (trade press)
- disposable income (consumer)/budget available (trade)
- where they live
- time they spend reading the publication
- political/religious/social affiliations.

Features start from an idea, which should suit the publication and interest the reader. There are few, if any, ideas that are new; the skill is in developing the brief. Two initial factors to consider: time and manageability. It's best to avoid round-up features of European academics in August, for example, because of the great escape from the heat of the cities; similarly, phone interviews with Singapore businessmen for a UK publication because of the time difference, unless you are able to work very early morning or late at night.

Ideas like 'Music in the movies' or 'Miscarriages of justice' aren't features, they're books. It's essential to slice them into manageable proportions, looking at trends in three recent British movie scores, for example, or examining four current justice campaigns. The more frequent the publication, the thinner the slice. Salami for dailies, toast for monthlies.

A well-thought-out brief provides direction and shape. Ideally it should include:

- deadline
- length
- the angle/approach you are adopting
- the tone (campaigning/informative/entertaining . . .)
- the scope/limits of the feature – what you plan to include/omit
- what's wanted: colourful quotes; background info; detailed facts; analysis . . .
- questions you want answered
- questions the editor wants answered
- where to go for research
- any extras: boxes, stat tables, pictures, illustrations.

Beware the editor/features editor who refuses to brief, saying airily 'You know what I want'. Experience shows they may have only a fuzzy notion of what they think they want but they know exactly what they *don't* want when they see it. Complex subjects must be thought through. If you are not given a brief, you should work one out, then go back and agree it with them.

A brief provides the basic structure and eases you into the next stage, research, which is a mammoth subject. Capsule advice is: start early, think laterally and, if you're stuck on sources, ask yourself 'In whose interest is it to hold this information?'

Research provides the bonus that editors prize: fresh facts, unexpected quotes, copy that elicits the 'never knew that' reaction. Don't skimp here. Make that extra phone call. Dig for that extra hour.

Interviewing comes next. Think, analyse, plan, focus as before and, if you're interviewing someone experienced at dealing with the press, try to make it interesting for them too, and remember they're well used to the wiles of journalists. Never ask celebrities the first question that springs to mind: it's likely to have sprung to every other mind as well. Celebrities apart, always ask obvious as well as stimulating questions.

With most feature subjects the skill is to get interviewees to drop their defences and talk. Go in/pick up the phone only when you're thoroughly prepared and you know exactly what you want to know. Don't talk too much; listen intently and intelligently to what's said; trade places and consider the impact of your questions.

Are you likely to get a good interview with a master of foxhounds if you start: 'How can you possibly be involved in such a contemptible business?' Be sceptical, not adversarial. Hostile questions can elicit good quotes but it's best to start nice and turn nasty later. Profile interviewers would do well to keep in mind the American saying 'You get more flies with honey than vinegar'.

Once you've completed the research and interviewing, pause. It's too soon to start writing. Best work out your plan first. You don't have to follow it slavishly, but forethought pays dividends and saves time.

One final, cynical observation: anyone who works for idiots will have to please idiots. You won't get into print if you don't.

INTROS

'It's no good standing there at the beginning of an article flexing your muscles. Just do the old handspring right away.'
'Cassandra', *Daily Mirror*

The subs and the editor are paid to read what you write; readers you have to grab. Most glance first at the headline, illustrations, maybe standfirst, and only then read the intro. You have about ten seconds in which to catch them.

> **Sesame Street** lied. America's not full of black and white kids, all learning together in multi-racial harmony. Down in LA, Big Bird's toting an AK and the Cookie Monster's doing crack.
> *Big Issue*

The power of this intro lies in its opening sentence, with the strong and unexpected verb 'lied'. '*Sesame Street* has been lying' wouldn't work as well.

The powerful start is followed with rich examples that conjure up funny, dramatic pictures. The rhythm of the last sentence works because it's in the right order, nailed down at the end by the single syllable 'crack'. It would be less effective if the Cookie Monster preceded Big Bird. If you doubt this, read the transposed sentence aloud.

> The groom fell asleep in his mother's lap. The bride burst into tears and had to be silenced with a piece of fruit. Dhanraj was four, his bride Santosh was seven. The wedding, which would change their lives forever, meant nothing to them. It was their parents who recited the marriage vows, their parents who circled the sacred fire seven times on their small and sleepy children's behalf.
> *Elle*

Here's another example of surprising juxtaposition, with the added ingredients of sex, judgement and strong images. The words are carefully chosen. 'Recited' has greater ceremonial overtones than 'repeated'. 'Silenced' rather than 'comforted' shows that something important is happening. 'The sacred fire' and 'seven' import mystic hints about a solemn ceremony which contrast with the touching 'small and sleepy children'.

There's no one way to write an intro, only the way that's right for the feature and the publication. The approach you select should spring from what you judge will most interest the reader. Content and style both have their part to play. The test of a good intro is that it grabs and keeps readers, so they read on.

Intros to avoid are those which bemuse, bore and activate the switch-off factor. So swap heads with the readers and avoid anything they could consider trite, banal, convoluted, negative, patronising or irrelevant; don't include too many sets of initials or, worst of all, write anything that can be dismissed with the comment 'So what?'

Types of intro

These five categories are useful as guides; in practice many excellent intros combine two or more elements.

1   Strong/provocative/intriguing statement
2   Narrative/anecdote
3   Description/scene-setting
4   Question that buttonholes the reader
5   Quote

1 Statement

Probably the most common way to start a feature, capable of almost infinite variation. Usually relies for impact on contrast, colour and surprise.

> We British still lead the world in something. Unfortunately, it's
> tabloid journalism.
> Adam Sweeting, *Guardian*

A straightforward, hard-to-resist first sentence. Opinionated second
sentence, spot-on for *Guardian* readers. It's a variation on the 'build 'em
up, knock 'em down' approach, with the punch words at the end.

> This week's deplorable idea comes from Crosse & Blackwell.
> *Times* Business Diary

That single judgemental adjective 'deplorable' does it. Very hard not to
read on to find out what the *Times* business diarist so reviled.

> Just when you thought it was safe to go back in the butcher's,
> it turns out that one very small brain is enough to make us all
> mad. The undersized organ belongs, of course, to Mr Jack
> Cunningham . . .
> Hugh Fearnley-Whittingstall, London *Evening Standard*

Starts with a stylish echo of the 'Jaws 2' sell-line that switches into
a comment on stratagems to combat the spread of BSE. Ends with a
triumphant 'gotcha!' as it becomes clear whose very small brain Fearnley-
Whittingstall refers to.

> As any tabloid newspaper can testify, there are three subjects
> guaranteed to revive a flagging circulation – diets, sex and royalty.
> With the Duchess of York, you get all three for the price of one . . .
> Francis Wheen, *Guardian*

Begins with deliberate polysyllabic pomposity: 'testify' instead of 'tell
you', 'revive a flagging circulation' rather than 'bring in new readers'.
Then this high-mindedness is brought down to earth with 'diets, sex and
royalty'. The pattern is repeated in the second sentence. No re-working
of the sentences can achieve the same impact.

> The Conservative Party conference is not what it used to be. The
> visitor to Bournemouth this week who looks for tribal continuity
> will still find it in the regulation blue rinses, the odd retired
> colonel and the half-witted ex-Oxbridge parliamentary candidates.
> However, the mass of the tribe has changed: the life and soul of the
> new Conservative Party, and the bed-rock of its support, is Essex
> man.
> *Sunday Telegraph*

This feature, the first to identify Essex Man, launched a way of seeing Conservative supporters for years. The intro starts with a simple statement, then turns descriptive. Bears all the signs of old-hand writing: analysis enlivened with specific stereotype images newly wrought, with 'blue rinses' standing for Tory matrons, 'half-witted . . . candidates' for the more clichéd Hooray Henrys. Fairly trite concepts, mass, tribe, life and soul, suddenly given more substance by 'bedrock' and the coining of the new 'Essex man'.

2 Narrative/anecdote

> According to a Chinese legend, a rich man commissions an artist to draw him a picture of a fish. Years pass by and the rich man grows impatient. He visits the artist and demands the picture or else he will cancel the deal.
>
> The artist then proceeds to draw the most exquisite fish of all time, in a mere 30 seconds. The rich man is well pleased but intensely puzzled. 'If you can produce something so beautiful in 30 seconds, how come I had to wait seven years?'
>
> The artist does not reply but instead leads the man over to a large cabinet which he opens to reveal several thousands of practice sketches of fishes.
>
> The Boat Race is similar to this . . .
> *Daily Telegraph*

An oblique intro, using a story – a device to use with care, as it can become trite or yukky, but, well chosen, can illustrate exactly what the writer intends.

> Haing Ngor shuddered as he watched the sun rise over the Cambodian slave village. By his side was the body of his malnour-ished wife, Chang My, who had died in agony before dawn. She had endured a 25-hour labour. Ngor's child died, too, trapped in the womb.
> *Daily Mail*

It's hard to resist the narrative pull of this gruesome story, simply told. This feature was pegged to news of the trial in Los Angeles of three men accused of murdering Haing Ngor, who won an Oscar for his part in the film *The Killing Fields*.

> The scene was Kitzbuhel, the programme Grandstand. The event was the Men's Downhill. A man referred to as 'Britain's sole

representative' came plummeting down the Streif. 'He won't be looking for a first place today,' said David Vine, 'he'll be looking for experience.'

At that very instant – not a bit later, but while David was actually saying it – Britain's sole representative was upside down and travelling into the crowd at 60mph plus. Spectators were mown down as if by grape-shot. The air was full of snow, beanies, mittens, bits of wood. You had to be watching to get the full impact. It was a kind of perfection.

Clive James, *Observer*

The first two matter-of-fact sentences set the scene and get the intro swinging along freely. The first hint of something out of the ordinary comes with 'A man referred to . . . ', which is taken up and echoed to great effect in the second paragraph. Consider, too, the use of the word 'plummeting'.

Is there any other word that would do as well? 'Plummet' comes from the French *plomb* for lead, and it gives the feeling of a headlong descent as the skier descends almost vertically. The well-placed quote follows, broken up with the attribution to the hapless David Vine so that the full weight of the sentence falls on the key word 'experience'.

The second paragraph begins plainly but after the first phrase, 'At that very instant', goes into 'freeze frame' or slow motion as the writer repeats what he said earlier but at greater length. This works because it mirrors what people involved in traffic accidents experience, using a device beloved of film-makers: that slowing down at moments of intensity.

Earlier the skier was allowed just the one action word 'plummeting' – now he's shown pictorially at greater length and the rest of the description works so well because it uses specific words: snow, beanies (bobble ski hats), mittens, bits of wood. All chosen to give the feeling of fragmentation and chaos.

I sat opposite Michael Parkinson at a charity dinner last winter and he looked bored out of his mind. The West End premiere that preceded it probably wasn't his cup of tea ('bloody hell' he muttered at one point). He winked once but for the most part lounged back in his black tie, maybe slightly squiffy, giving an impression of girth, of spent success, at any rate exuding the comfortable aloofness of the most famous person at the table. Occasionally, he would wander off and Mary Parkinson would peal, 'Where's the old silver fox gone now?'

> It was a very different Michael Parkinson I met the other day in a green room at Television Centre to promote the return of Parkinson, hitting your screens again after 15 years.
> Sabine Durrant, *Guardian*

Before and After anecdotes. Before: self-satisfied, replete, disengaged. Well chosen, judgemental and deliberately dated words: 'squiffy', 'girth', 'spent success' – he seems past it, he's given up caring. After: well, you have to read on. Parky as supplicant for publicity. A feature that celebrities' agents would do well to file, then check if their clients had met Sabine Durrant before somewhere.

> Jack Dee is assiduously polite to the girl who serves him a cappuccino at his London club. He smiles, moves aside any clutter from the table and says 'thank-you' twice. When she leaves he comments on how good the service is. It is something he always notices. He has never forgotten his days as a waiter.
> *Daily Express* Saturday magazine

Deceptively simple 'we were there' start that reveals more than the usual writer and celeb meet and talk intro, through the detailed retelling of Dee's behaviour.

3 Description/scene-setting

> The door is flung open and a tiny tornado sweeps through it. Lickety-spit. High heels on parquet. Clickety click. Bangles a-jangle. The blur of beige safari suiting resolves itself into Joan Collins wearing flared knee-length shorts, waistcoat and jacket. Her hair is tied back and covered with a fine-weave hat with a deep brim. From beneath it, scarlet lips break into a wide, welcoming smile.
> *Options*

Active, staccato, colourful. Those who like alliteration and sentence fragments will enjoy this, with its deliberate evocation of Joan Collins's flamboyance through image and assonance. Just as it's harder to write short than long, it's more difficult to get across approval than scorn. Notable for use of actual colour words and the good strong verbs, particularly in the first sentence. This intro starts with the prose equivalent of the 'medium' shot in film, then uses 'jump cutting' techniques. Done with panache, as here, it adds lustre to a publication. Badly done, it's deeply embarrassing, so be careful.

> Clutching a cigarette in his left hand and taking occasional gulps from a modified version of the Wimbledon barley-water tray with

his right, Jocky Wilson became darts champion of the world at Stoke-on-Trent on Saturday.

Thus a planet that already has the odd champion with no hair and a great many with no brains, finally acquired one with no teeth.
Matthew Engel, *Guardian*

The pleasure is in the second sentence, despite its starting with the archaic 'Thus'. Perfectly pointed 'triplet' writing which employs specific, concrete words to great cumulative effect – hair, brains and teeth. There's extra joy to be derived from remembered images of bald and brainless champions.

(A feature on a de-tox programme run by Buddhist monks in Thailand.)

It's a tidal wave of puke. Like a line of wells simultaneously striking oil, fountains of sick erupt from the mouths of the four drug addicts. The clear fluid arcs four feet through the air and splatters the earth before the kneeling junkies.
Maxim

Targeted at *Maxim*'s body-function-obsessed readers. Visual rather than smell-oriented, thank goodness. Lots of movement words: sick 'erupts', fluid 'arcs' and 'splatters'. Keeps to the vernacular with 'puke' and 'sick' rather than 'vomit'.

If the fashion industry eats its young, Jeremy Scott is ready to bite back. When we meet in Paris, he's wearing gold fronts on his top teeth, with the incisors extended into vampire fangs and his name etched on the metal – not that you're likely to forget it, because Scott is hot. A telling handful of the industry's tastemakers have anointed this farm boy from the American Midwest as the Next Big Thing.
Scene

A muted description which doesn't need any extra adjectives to conjure a bizarre picture, with all the hype left to judgement.

Every cold, damp January for 15 years the reminder has been there: a lingering ache in my left shoulder, which came from queuing up for seven hours in the bitter cold outside an undistinguished villa at Neauphle-le-Chateau, near Paris. I couldn't move in case I lost my place to one of the hundreds of eager Iranian students behind me. The villa was Ayatollah Khomeini's headquarters, and we were waiting to join his flight back to Tehran from exile – a 15-year exile. My office in London had instructed me not to go, but I decided to

go anyway. How often do you get the chance to watch a revolution
at first hand?
John Simpson, *Guardian*

This is a crafty piece of story-telling, a physically descriptive narrative.
Almost every phrase sets up questions that pull the reader further into the
story. A 'reminder' was there. Why? What reminder? A 'lingering ache' –
Why lingering? Where was the ache? Not just in his shoulder but
specifically in his left shoulder. 'Queuing up for seven hours . . .' Why?
An undistinguished chateau. Why undistinguished? Indicates the value
of long years of 'writing to camera'. Writing in pictures works just as well
for features.

> When the kid in the front row at the rally bit off the tip of his little
> finger and wrote KIM DAE JUNG in blood on his fancy white ski
> jacket – I think that was the first time I ever really felt like a foreign
> correspondent. I mean, here was something really fucking *foreign*.
> P J O'Rourke, *Rolling Stone*

Straight in at the deep end with a bizarre incident. Take the 'fancy white'
out of the description of the jacket and the intro doesn't work so well
– the blood loses much of its colour. Unerringly sets the scene for a
violent review of South Korean elections, which ends with his getting
tear-gassed.

4 Question that buttonholes the reader

Designed to intrigue and make the reader think. The question needs to be
right for the readers, or it runs the risk of a 'couldn't-care-less' response.

> Why is it that as women become champs in the boardroom, so
> many of them become chumps in the bedroom?
> *Glamour*

Feminists may shudder, but this economically written intro, with its use
of assonance and contrast: 'champs' and 'chumps', 'boardroom' and 'bedroom', – was spot on for *Glamour*'s readers. They *did* want to know why.

> Do you have an annual appraisal system? Why? Before expending
> energy on a process so complicated and potentially controversial,
> it makes sense to ask what you hope to achieve. Most businesses
> do not know why they have one. They just do.
> *Accountancy*

Barristers, it's said, ask witnesses questions in court only when they know what the answer will be. Writers can't be certain how readers will reply. One device is the immediate follow-up question. The joy here is that whether the answer to the first is Yes or No, the second question is still valid. Great final sentence, making the writer's point with the print equivalent of a despairing shrug of the shoulders.

> Where would the actress Amanda Donohoe prefer to be today? Anywhere else, I would guess, than in the Groucho Club having lunch with me . . .
> Andrew Billen, *Observer*

This is the print equivalent of 'Fasten your seatbelts – we're in for a bumpy ride.' It was an entertaining and revealing interview but Billen had to work hard and include more clippings-generated copy than usual.

> Even at this time of triumph it is important to remember the verities of cricket between England and Australia. Winning is not what matters; the Ashes are about renewing old friendships in a spirit of sporting endeavour between two nations with a common bond. But, by God, isn't it great to beat the bastards?
> Matthew Engel, *Guardian*

It's the tone of voice that does it. At the start, mouthing plummy, treacly platitudes commonly employed to make defeat more acceptable: 'the verities of cricket' . . . 'winning is not what matters' . . . 'renewing old friendships in a spirit of sporting endeavour'. Then suddenly there's a whoop of joy as the writer switches accents out of received English pronunciation and into Strine: 'Isn't it great to beat the bastards?' Again, the punch word is in the punch position.

5 Quote

The most controversial of intro types. Variously damned and dismissed as lazy and/or confusing for the reader, and typographically difficult for the sub. In its favour: a good quote can be very effective and, if accompanied by a whopping big picture of the subject, it's a strange reader who would be confused. Best used sparingly. The prejudice against quotes is rooted more strongly in newspapers than magazines.

> 'I remember that I first became an adulteress to the sound of Mozart.'
>
> The sentence stops a reader in his tracks.

> Especially when it is autobiographical and the writer a dis-
> tinguished public figure.
> London *Evening News*

A great quote. Does it matter that the readers don't know who's talking? That's the point. Who is this famous woman using such archaic language?

> 'Sex, lust, greed, hate, revenge,' says Susan Howatch promptly,
> when asked what her books are about, by interviewers who have
> not actually read them.
> *Times*

Another great quote, this time neatly set in context so that the reader is not misled. Who says lists are boring?

> Gillian Helfgott, wife of the controversial pianist David Helfgott,
> says she doesn't give a hoot about the critics. Not a hoot. In fact
> she spends an hour telling me she doesn't give a hoot. During
> which time it becomes quite clear that she gives many hoots. She
> loathes them, despises them, detests them, thinks them spineless,
> passionless, loveless, worthless. 'You tell me, who has done more
> for classical music, David Helfgott or the critics?' She jabs her
> finger into my chest. I don't have to think too hard about the
> answer.
>
> It is midnight. It has been a long evening. But she is relentless. This
> is one tough cookie . . .
> Stephen Moss, *Guardian*

Reported speech: a safer way to use a quote if you work for an anti-quote-start paper. This is musical writing that uses repeated *leit motifs*, first all those 'hoots', then loads of 'less/es' remorselessly piling up. The later quote lightens the accumulated adjectives, which contrast with the strong 'jabs'. The final sentence of the first par works so well because you pick up her imperiousness, a feeling of being there, listening to her tirade, feeling the jab.

One final way to start with a quote. Leave out the quote marks.

> I'm getting a bit sick of your apoplectic roarings, wrote a male
> reader last week.
>
> I do seem to have been rumbling of late like a 15-stone belligerent
> battle-axe, so this week I will enchant, enslave and delight you with
> something merry and light like marital rows.
> Lynda Lee-Potter, *Daily Mail*

CONTENT

You've grabbed them with the intro. Now you've got to keep them reading. The care and effort that go into each word of the opening should continue through to the end.

Feature contents are determined by the brief and split into four categories. First, information: details on people and things, including facts and background 'colour'. Second, anecdotes. Third, quotes. Fourth, assessment, analysis, opinion. All can co-exist in one paragraph, of course. Then there are sundry devices to add spice and ways to link contents together.

1 Information

Some features are briefed to be fact-heavy and the details you include depend on your judgement of what will interest the readers. Readability depends on how you present those facts: loosely packed or indigestibly squashed.

> [Of the special effects created for the film] Chief among them, of course, was a replica of the Titanic. Or rather several of them. Even a 1/20 scale model was over 45ft long. There was a 25ft version just to work out camera angles; there was one of the weed-encrusted wreck – which was hung upside down from a ceiling to make filming it easier. Shots of it were laced into shots of the real wreck.
>
> But the big ship, the one that counted, was built along a sandy strip of beach in Mexico, and it was, near as damn it, full-sized. It must have been an extraordinary sight to see its vast, weird outline riding the waterfront sands. The Titanic was, in its day, the largest moving object ever made. The reproduction can claim to be the largest film prop ever made. It was 775ft long – 90 per cent full size – and for obvious reasons it had to be made able to tilt.
>
> The real Titanic, best iron and steel as she was, couldn't take the weight of having her back end lifted out of the water; it broke as she sank so the reproduction had to be made stronger, because it had to be tilted and lowered dozens of times without real loss of life. Three-and-a-half million tons of steel and 15,000 sheets of plywood went into it . . .
> *Daily Mail* Weekend magazine

Fact-packed – twenty-four by my count in the first two pars – but not dense. The writing is airy with not a backward reference or sub-clause preceding the subject anywhere except in that rather awkward first sentence. Most of the figures are round numbers, an aid to understanding in consumer writing.

If the feature is to be fact heavy, try to spread the information throughout, rather than bunch it. Alternatively, put very detailed information into boxes to accompany the article (see 'Extras' section, page 86).

Sometimes in fact-heavy writing, lists are unavoidable, but items listed baldly can be tedious. It's much better to describe in detail. Here's an example of how grabbing vivid specifics can be.

> [Harold Nicolson] noticed everything – pauses, tics, hand move-ments . . . There's an instance . . . when he had to take an urgent despatch to Lord Curzon in his bedroom at Carlton House Terrace. He can't have been there more than a few minutes but, by the time he leaves, the room is indelibly video-taped in his head – the cheap washbasin painted with cornflowers; the Pears soap; the thin, scruffy shaving brush; the stained wooden hairbrush; the old Gladstone bag in a corner; the washing bill on the mantelpiece.
> John Carey, *Sunday Times*

There's no necessity for the list to be unusual.

> Periodically I get exercise kicks. I also dream of reading the entire works of Shakespeare, learning the Bible by heart, becoming fluent in Russian and Chinese, learning to drive a car, baking all my own bread, etc.
> *Daily Mail*

Every one is a cliché – that's why it works, down to the 'etc.'.

Well-chosen specific words are sensuous. Because they have 'handles', i.e. are graspable, they reach readers in a way concepts don't. Here's a GP writing about poverty and violence in the East End of London. Correction, about his experience of poor and violent men and women. Correction, what he has seen, felt, heard, touched, smelt.

> When I came [to the East End] I didn't know what the bruised face of a raped heroin addict was like, or how children could be locked up without food, four in a room by a drunken father as a punish-ment, or what happens to a jaw when it is broken in a domestic fight and concealed. Now I do. I know what decomposed bodies of alcoholics smell like after two weeks, and the noises made when dying in pain and what happens to a woman's face when she is told her breast cancer has spread. I wish I didn't.
> David Widgery, *Guardian*

The rhythmic writing falls into two sections. First there's a powerful list of three – bruised face, locked-up children and broken jaw – followed by a short factual sentence: 'Now I do.' Next another list of three but all involving death – decomposed bodies, dying noises, woman's face – followed by a more passionate variation of the first coda: 'I wish I didn't.' The powerful images need no extra adjectives.

> Marco Pierre White, fat hands waving, pale brown eyes staring . . .
> has been awake all night, 20 hours in a solicitor's office discussing
> a 'huge deal' and you can smell his armpits a table away.
> Katharine Viner, *Guardian*

Nice catering touch: 'a table away'.

Visual metaphors, conjured by just one or two words, are equally powerful. Here's Laline Paull writing about tycoon Jimmy Goldsmith after his death.

> Even before I knew of his affinity with predators, I privately classi-
> fied him as a king crocodile – a vast and glinting smile, a lazy gait
> and an impenetrable mask of politeness. But very, very dangerous.
> *Guardian*

King crocodile is a cruel comparison requiring explanation, which she provides chillingly. 'Glinting' contains real menace and 'mask' is much more frightening than 'veneer'. This is a picture that sticks in the memory, writing that changes perception.

The journalistic skills required to write for the trade press are the craft basics, but the application and thinking differ, particularly when writing main body copy. Trade press writing is neglected in books about journalism, probably because the examples don't make easy or exciting reading.

But trade journalists deserve recognition for their skill. Their readers are experts, so writing for them is demanding and stimulating. Superficial generalisations won't do. Intelligent analysis, reliable, fresh facts and statistics are wanted.

> A different approach to CPU acceleration comes from DayStar,
> whose much-acclaimed range of accelerators work with just about
> every Mac going. They fit into the Processor Direct Slot (PDS) on
> your Mac's motherboard. This means you don't need a free NuBus
> slot, and the simpler configuration means that DayStar confidently
> offers a '100 percent compatible' guarantee with its cards. There

are a range of Power-Cache cards which use a 68030 processor
(like a MacIIci) . . .
Jo Francis, *XYZ*

You may not know what it means but XYZ's readers did and acquired the
information easily, because of the way it's written.

Trade publications have their industry 'must know' facts, which should
be included whenever relevant. In writing about hotels, for example,
required information includes location, number of rooms, number of
beds, occupancy rates, tariffs, category, staff by function (front-of-house,
housekeeping, waiting, etc.), gross profit margin, banqueting facilities,
etc. For wine producers, for example, hectarage, grape types, production
by volume (hectolitres) with percentage increase/decrease over past
years, export figures by volume and value with percentage increase/
decrease over selected years, outlets, campaign spends, etc.

The 'magic of the product' info, such a feature of consumer briefing, is
absent or, if present, is heavily questioned. The skill here is understanding the business well enough to latch on to what will grab the
readers.

> In the basement of the old market were bungarouch walls: a
> local speciality built by setting courses of pebbles in lime mortar.
> Although bungarouch has a reputation for crumbling if exposed to
> damp, Johnson says that, even in the basement, the walls proved
> as strong as blockwork.
> *Building*

By contrast with consumer press writing, statistics must be as exact as
possible. Here's a par from a feature on production, imports and sales
of tufted carpets in the UK.

> Ex-manufacturer prices of UK-produced tufted carpets have
> increased [in each of the last three years] by more than the rate
> of inflation. This is because manufacturers have been trading up,
> preferring to produce more quality tufted carpet in an effort to
> improve profitability.
>
> Last year the average price per sq m was £5.88 – exactly 5 per cent
> higher than the previous year. The value of UK tufted production at
> ex-manufacturer prices increased from £535.7m in 1995 to £575.7m
> in 1996, but last year fell back to £570.9m.
> *Carpet and Floorcoverings Review*

2 Anecdotes

One good anecdote is worth columns of description. This was collected first-person and stored for years.

> Since everyone else recited their favourite Maxwell story last week, let me give you mine. Shortly after he dawn-raided the bankrupt British Printing Corporation in the early 1980s, I invited him to lunch in my office. Still persona non grata in the City after the DTI's savage condemnation of him, he was typically bouncing back and wanted bank support.
>
> An hour before lunch he rang, down a suitably crackly line. 'I'm sorry I can't make your lunch,' he boomed. 'I'm in Bucharest.'
>
> I said I was sorry to hear it, particularly as there were going to be some other interesting people there. Who were they, he inquired. Two bankers, I replied, Philip Wilkinson of NatWest and John Quinton of Barclays.
>
> 'You've got Wilkinson and Quinton, have you? Give me a moment.' The line went dead, then he was back on. 'I'll be round there in 10 minutes.' And he was.
> Ivan Fallon, *Sunday Times*

Tells more about Maxwell than long accounts of his financial affairs. The anecdote swings along, describing what happened with no added frills except 'boomed' and 'suitably crackly', which prove their value later. The end is beautifully judged. Good anecdotes require no editorialising.

> When Kitty Kelley was researching her unauthorised biography of Frank Sinatra she was told the singer had recently bought $200,000 worth of furniture in cash in wrapping paper from a Las Vegas casino – an indication of Sinatra's links with the gaming industry.
>
> She found a friend who bore a resemblance to Sinatra. Kelley then had her own hair done to match that of Sinatra's wife Barbara. Together, Kelley and her friend went to the furniture store. They told the sales assistant that they had heard that Frank Sinatra had bought some furniture from the store. Indeed he had, said the salesman.
>
> Well, said Kelley, they were so fond of the singer they modelled themselves on him, right down to their looks and lifestyle. They had to have the same furniture for their home, which was an exact copy of his. What did he buy? The proud salesman rattled off the

list. We will take it, said Kelley. Because we follow his life to the letter, we must pay the way he did – so how did he pay? Which credit card did he use?

The salesman produced the payslip. Cash. Come on, honey, said Kelley, clutching her companion, we must go to Las Vegas and get the cash. They left the store and never returned. She had her story . . .
Chris Blackhurst, *Independent on Sunday*

The style here is speech reported rather than reported speech, a device which enables the reader to hear the conversation as it might have happened, rather than the reported speech approach ('Kelley then told the salesman that they were devoted fans of Sinatra, modelling their appearance and lifestyle on him and would like to obtain the same furniture that he had bought.') One tiny complaint: 'her own hair'? 'Her hair' would do.

Short anecdotes can be equally telling. From an obit of Violet Carlson, the Broadway dancer:

She once broke her wrist playing in the Jerome Kern musical *Sweet Adeline*, had it set in plaster and was back on stage before the end of the performance.
Guardian

3 Quotes

What people say brings vitality to copy, relieves solid text, changes pace and offers a fresh or authoritative voice, allowing the interviewee to speak. In most features a quote early on acts as a 'kicker', enlivening serious introductions or detailed scene-setting.

Unlike news writers, who attribute quotes at the beginning or end of the sentence, feature writers – as ever – have more choice. They can break up the quote to show it to best advantage. The placing of 'she says' below enables the strongest words to occupy the most important position in the sentence.

'The foot,' she says, 'is an architectural masterpiece.'
Financial Times

Writers can animate an ordinary quote with description, movement, colour, which act like stage directions.

'If I was doing a 30-second piece to camera right now,' says the twinkly, rumpled man sprawled on the park bench, 'I would get into a completely obsessed state. No really, that's true.' He sits up and leans forward, insistent. 'I'm as nervous now, before every single thing I do, as I was the day I did my first piece of television.'

It is hard to think of a less plausible thing for David Dimbleby to say . . .
Decca Aitkenhead, *Guardian*

When a quote is less than hoped for, context can give meaning.

Did she use memories of her father's death to help her performance? 'Yes, I did. Of course. You draw on whatever you have,' she says briskly. Silence. I can see her wondering if there isn't something more urgent she should be doing . . .
Kristin Scott Thomas interviewed in the *Sunday Times* magazine

Questionnaires are a specialised form of feature. Studying the better examples provides a great guide to using quotes, shortened and pointed, to maximum effect.

What's the worst piece of gossip you've ever read about yourself?

The Sun once listed '20 Things You Didn't Know About Barry Norman' and there were at least ten things that *I* didn't know about Barry Norman.
Barry Norman, *Empire*

What would you like written on your tombstone?

Unavailable. Please try me on the mobile.
Mel Smith, *Empire*

Edited quotes are often smoother than usual speech patterns. The general guideline is the longer the quote, the more cutting and combining is necessary.

My children came up to the bedroom and said the Teletubbies weren't on the TV, so I knew that something Very Important had happened. I had until four the next afternoon, our deadline, to produce a humorous magazine. It was about as hard as it's got for me, but when I read Monday's papers I knew what my reaction was and what the magazine had to do. The speed with which grief turned into self-righteousness – an angry self-righteousness, perhaps born of guilt – I really hated that. We were witnessing the biggest U-turn in media history, with the press pretending that their behaviour over the past ten years simply hadn't happened.

Ian Hislop on events after the death of Diana, Princess of Wales, quoted by Ian Jack, *Granta*

4 Assessment, analysis, opinion

Have something to say and say it well. 'Benjamin Spock was one of the most influential doctors of the 20th century.' Ordinary. The day after he died, one appreciation read:

> When the rollcall of the men and women who shaped the 20th century is finally read, Benjamin Spock will be way up the list.

Much better. 'Rollcall' carries with it hints of a day of judgement.

The journalistic aside is a useful device for the sure-footed. Here's Lynn Barber at her best in the *Observer* in 1997, interviewing Kelvin MacKenzie. The comment – you'll know it when you get there – is an example of personality breaking through brilliantly.

> My colleagues keep telling me not to be soft on Kelvin. Soft? The truth is I'm squishy on Kelvin, I regard him as probably the greatest newspaper genius of my lifetime. John Sweeney tries to stiffen my sinews by reminding me of Kelvin's crimes at the *Sun* – printing a photograph of the vicarage rape victim on the front page, running a phoney interview with a Falklands widow and calling it a 'world exclusive', printing 'the Truth' about the Hillsborough tragedy, which wasn't the truth at all. Sir Nicholas Lloyd, former editor of the *Daily Express*, tells me to ask him how he feels about ruining the reputation of British journalism for a decade. Oh, pooh. I believe Kelvin's *Sun*, his currant bun, was the wittiest, brightest, boldest newspaper in the history of the world and that, despite his occasional serious errors of judgement (see 'crimes' above), he almost single-handedly kept the newspaper-reading habit alive in the British working class. I used to get furious with people who said the *Sun* was vulgar. Of course it was vulgar. What do you expect your plumber to read – the *Independent*? But it was also funny and cheerful and life-enhancing, and kept politicians in their place. And now Kelvin is managing director of a dim television channel that hardly anyone watches. What a waste.

Sundry devices

Film techniques can work well in journalism. The following intro starts with a close-up, then pulls back to a medium shot and puts the feature in context.

> One warm, sunny evening three weeks ago, I found myself lying on the floor of a house in north London pointing my camera at a strange man's genitals. I wasn't alone. Beside me, a middle-aged woman was kneeling with her head poised inches away from his groin, tongue lolling in concentration while she captured on film some anatomical nuance. Positioned around the edges of the backdrop, other women – among them an anthropologist, an executive for a pharmaceuticals company, the former editor of a women's porn magazine . . . were halfway up stepladders or crouched on the floor, shutters racing.
> *Guardian*

One fact as embodiment of the person is a variation of the one person as embodiment of a story approach (see 'Structure', over) but more economical.

From a feature on the retiring head of American Airlines:

> A fierce cost-cutter who once saved $100,000 by removing olives from all AA's salads . . .
> *Economist*

As features get shorter this device grows in value, but the detail must tell.

Go with the flow

The best way to ensure a feature flows smoothly from start to finish is to turn yourself into the reader and, while writing, to keep going back to the top and reading it *right through* to yourself – as though for the first time – to check that nothing is ambiguous or mystifying, that sentences are not too long and that the rhythm is right.

To do this, you should sound the words, albeit silently, in your head. And re-read not just once or twice, but every time you pause, whether it's to check a fact, answer the phone or stare out of the window. Most lumpen writing is a result of lumpen ears, an inability to empathise and/or not reading your own copy from the top.

How to link is a much disputed area. Smooth flowing copy is one thing, lousy links are another and very off-putting. For almost all features, say what you want to say in an order that makes sense progressively, returning to a previously made point or subject only if you can prove relevance or illustrate progress. This is where reading what you've written to yourself is invaluable.

To smooth the reader's path, try to ensure the first sentence of each paragraph gives some clue to what the par's about. The classic, formulaic way to link is to repeat at the start of a par some word or words that occurred in the previous par. (See the Matthew Engel feature, pages 90–2.) Overdone this makes for weary reading. Echoing a word, thought or idea works better.

Links are particularly necessary in 'on the one hand and on the other' features, where opposing views have to be balanced. You'll find there such linking phrases as:

> A more serious worry is . . .
> Criticisms of the product focus on . . .
> The roots of the problem run much deeper . . .
> So what is being done to reverse the trend?

Rules, they say, are made for the guidance of wise men and the observance of fools – that's why guidelines is the preferred word throughout. If you have to make a sudden switch, just do it and take consolation that, if hooked, the reader will follow, no matter how difficult the leap.

STRUCTURE

Of all the stages in feature writing, structure is the most difficult. The brief may be the most neglected, but its requirements are clear and, once followed, provide a workable guide to what is wanted. The material gathered may differ from what was planned but the task of structuring remains the same: to select what's relevant and integrate it into a smooth-running whole.

This is not easy and short-cut solutions have been devised which bypass the need to learn to structure: putting copy into chart form or a pre-agreed layout – four quotes, an intro and a box, for example. Speedy, uncomplicated, but no help when it comes to writing long text features.

These are more complex than news stories and are crafted as a unit, with a beginning, middle and end. Paragraphs are not written in descending order of importance, cuttable from the end: the pyramid doesn't apply.

Trainee journalists naturally look for a formula to follow and many become uneasy when they can't find one to suit all features. They need to accept that solutions have to be custom made.

Editors whose writers use a single template soon spot it and sigh 'Here we go again, starting with a quote . . . '. Or 'Not another "There I woz with . . . "'. The design to adopt is the one that is right for that feature for that publication.

Where to begin?

Planning is critical. The more complex the feature, the longer you should take, making sure you are in complete control of your subject before you start. This enables you to get an overview. Begin writing too early and you'll find yourself struggling through the elephant grass, unable to see where you're going.

What follows works for even the most complex subjects and ultimately saves time. First, go back to your brief. If you discover gaps, plug them. Then read and re-read your research and interview notes until you have assimilated them. During this process, information on various aspects of the feature should be drawn together.

Take a subject like 'Successful fund-raising', with the angle 'making it profitable and fun'. Interviews with several practised fund-raisers might yield information on events that provide maximum income from minimum effort, advice on motivating helpers, tips on planning enjoyable campaigns, suggestions on recruiting committee members, crazy ideas that children like, warnings about legal requirements and details of helpful books.

These become headings, under which each fund-raiser's thoughts are collated. A good way to do this is to use a variant of the 'mind map'. Take a large sheet of blank paper, A3 if possible, and in the middle put a drawing or representation of the subject to help focus the mind, then scatter your headings anywhere. This is important because it liberates the writer from the tyranny of linear thinking. Ring each heading boldly, leaving plenty of space, and, as you go through your notes, add the most interesting quotes, facts, whatever, under each relevant heading.

When you've done this and taken the measure of your possible contents, you can then decide what you are going to say. To achieve this, answer a key question. How you phrase it doesn't matter. It can be any variation on:

- What's the storyline?
- What do I want the readers to take away from this feature?
- What's the point I want to make?

This focuses the mind and stops the essay approach, which starts with the task about to be undertaken not the conclusion reached. If in doubt, rehearse to yourself the subject, publication and readers.

For example: 'I'm writing a feature on . . . [insert subject] for . . . [insert publication] whose readers are . . . [insert a generalised description] and what I want to them to take away is . . . ' This helps establish how relevant your approach is.

If yours sounds like 'I'm writing a feature on Lasham Airfield during WW2 for *Historic Hampshire*, whose readers are residents keen on local history, and what I want to tell them about is the current employment situation on the airfield and concern about glider noise', you're clearly on the wrong track.

Don't start typing yet

When you know what you want to say, work out a running order that will carry the reader with you from A to Z. To do this, look at all your source material, now collected under various headings, and choose where to start. Bearing in mind your 'take away' factor, swap heads with the reader and decide what will best bait the hook. What's

- the most startling fact you've discovered?
- the best anecdote unearthed?
- the most astonishing quote?
- the most surprising event?
- the item with the greatest 'Hey, did you know that . . . ?' factor?

This is where understanding the readers' priorities meshes with editorial policy to become invaluable. Once you have decided where to start – not necessarily having written the intro in your head – where next?

One way is to look at the ringed headings and plot the feature's progress with arrows and links, talking it through to yourself, so that the topics flow smoothly. It's important to keep information on topics together and not to jump around all over the place.

After being told this, an American journalist commented: 'My first reaction was "obviously", my second "but why didn't it ever occur to me?" and my third that it was one of those profound banalities "everyone knows – after they've been told."'

Some writers number each piece of research and then adopt the Chinese takeaway approach: 'I'll start with 19, go on to 45, 102, 93, 4, 8 . . . '. This takes a very particular mind-set. Others go effortlessly from reading their notes to making a simple list. This is difficult, so be careful.

Well crafted, a feature can be a must-follow yellow brick road; badly done, it becomes a confusing maze of dead-end, unappealing streets without signposts. Readers will following meandering paths or four-lane highways if the way is interesting and well marked. They stop reading if confused.

Clive James's first job on the Sydney *Morning Herald* was rewriting 'casuals' (amateur contributions). 'Those months doing rewrites,' he says, 'were probably the best practical training I ever received . . . Gradually the sheer weight of negative evidence began to convince me that writing is essentially a matter of saying things in the right order.'

Three-way split

Features have a beginning, a middle and an end:

1   Intro, start, top (contains the hook)
2   Main body copy
3   Ending.

In the simplest features, the hook leads effortlessly into the main body copy. This can contain any number of sections, smoothly linked, which take the reader right through to the ending, which wraps up the feature.

But what if the feature is to aid understanding of the financial difficulties of Nicaragua, explain new developments in leasehold property law or demonstrate the results of taxation inequalities on booze between England and France – all of which, stated like that, make unappealing hooks? A link must be forged between the hook and the main body copy.

Enter the nub par, also called the anchor par, pivot par, 'dear reader' par, which tells the reader what the feature is about. In features on obscure or complicated subjects there may also be a context par, setting out any necessary background.

Let's start with two complex feature examples, then everything else will seem simple. Here's a *Financial Times* feature on the Chinese economy. It starts with a descriptive, 'person as embodiment of the story' hook, using contrast.

> The herdsman stood by a stream near mountains that fell away like a Chinese painting. But when he was told he lived in a beautiful area, his face darkened.
>
> 'Beautiful is beautiful, but life here is poor,' he said. The price of his six cows had fallen by two-thirds in the past two years and he planned to sell them all this autumn. 'I'm getting out of herding. I'll be free,' he added.

Context par follows, putting the example into the wider macro-economic picture.

> His condition is common right across China, not only among some 900m people who live off the land but also in primary industries and even among manufacturers making successful new Chinese brands.

Now the nub par, indicating the scope of the feature.

> Seven consecutive months of falling prices, driven by chronic oversupply, have slashed profit margins and forced farmers and corporations to rein in future output. The deflationary trend is not new, but it appears to be accelerating.

Main body copy follows, pars on:

> overview of Asian deflationary pressures
> China's deflation, statistical indications
> government spending figures
> foreign investment
> reform of state enterprises.

The ending covers reflationary plans.

Variations of the person-as-embodiment-of-the-story are anecdote as embodiment, and event and detail as embodiment.

The second *Financial Times* example starts with a 'colour' hook, involving a corny play on words.

> Wim Kok, the Dutch prime minister, tugged manfully at a rowing machine. Frits Bolkestein and Jaap de Hoop Scheffer, his two main rivals, respectively wielded a tennis racquet and jogged on a treadmill. At an event convened last month by the country's heart foundation, each wanted to show he was fit for government.

Context pars:

> Fitness in the eyes of the voters will be decided in a general election today. This follows a campaign which has by no means quickened the national pulse.
>
> As a series of inconclusive televised debates wound up and photo opportunities dwindled, the lunchtime news on the state-owned network yesterday devoted not a moment to domestic or European politics.

Nub par: this is why the reader should read on.

> But the choice the Dutch will make, as the first Europeans to vote since the single currency became a certainty, will help determine the economic course of a core participant in monetary union. And electoral sentiment is shifting leftward.

Main body copy follows. Each section contains one or more pars on:

> prospects for the left-wing parties
> prospects for the free-market liberals
> prospects for the right-wing parties
> coalition possibilities.

Conclusion: Kok's Blair-like efforts to bolster his chances.

Next a feature on two teams battling it out in the 'University Challenge' final, which involved considerable research. Starts with 'disaster' hook reinforced by emotive words, detail and anecdote.

> Only a year ago, they were a laughing stock after slumping to the biggest defeat in the history of TV's University Challenge.
>
> Crushed by 360 points to 40, Birkbeck College, London, found themselves the butt of student bar jibes and even elicited the sympathy of normally hard-nosed quizmaster Jeremy Paxman.

'Nub' or 'pivot' par. All is changed. Readers can expect to learn why/how.

> Sixteen months on, however, things could not be more different.

Context pars which dramatise present situation:

> On Tuesday night on BBC2, after the greatest comeback in the show's 36-year history, Birkbeck will lock brains with reigning champions Magdalen College, Oxford, in the 1998 final.
>
> And the four-strong team are determined finally to bury the memory of that humiliation at the hands of Manchester University.

Main body copy starts. The first section fleshes out the team: quotes the captain; includes details about college and team members; explains how the previous team was chosen.

Second 'nub par' introduces second body copy section:

> This year the selection process was far more rigorous.

Second section contains details about selection and training. Cut to action for third section, reliving progress to the final.

'Nub sentence' introduces fourth section:

> The final will be an intriguing contest of town versus gown.

The fourth section contrasts the opposing colleges, then builds up to the ending, which echoes the first par and moves to a positive conclusion.

> But win or lose, Birkbeck will have restored their reputation.
> *Mail on Sunday*

Red-top tabloids write on complex subjects too, but use specific examples most of the time to illustrate.

Hook – you're there witnessing blatant crime (on a massive scale), followed by detail:

On any day of the week you can walk along the front at Dover and see, unfolding before your eyes, the biggest criminal enterprise in Britain.

Battered vans spill from the docks, laden with cheap booze and tobacco. Within days they will be hawked around clubs, factory gates and housing estates as far away as Manchester and Glasgow.

Nub par:

Every load is another nail in the coffin of the traditional British pub. On an average day, three pubs close down for good.

First section, detailing what sort of pubs and why they're under threat:

Those most likely to disappear are small locals that help hold communities together. For years they have been hammered by social changes and brewery rationalisation.

Now the bootleggers are poised to finish them off. The amount of beer coming across the Channel each day equals the weekly sales of 1,000 pubs.

Most of it sells for less than two thirds of the cheapest super-market price.

Second section: history of modern bootlegging. Third section: present situation. Fourth section: personalising the story.

Alan Bridgewater, landlord of the Bridge End Inn at Govilon, South Wales, says: 'I'm losing seven per cent of my beer sales to the bootleggers. For a small pub that can make the difference between staying afloat and going out of business.

'Every landlord I know is affected. The stuff is everywhere.'

It's even worse in the big cities.

Three examples follow.

Late 'context par': the conflict spelled out. The nitty-gritty of excise duty, tax, etc.: Solution signalled with warning of results of inertia.

The core of the problem is that Britain's beer is taxed at 32p a pint – six times the rate in France. Our tobacco is taxed four times more heavily than Belgium.

A bootlegger with a Transit van can make £600 profit a trip. And some gangs make ten trips a day. . . .

> But Britain has refused to cut its high taxes on tobacco and booze, citing health concerns and the loss of money to the Exchequer. Yet some experts believe the economy would actually gain from a duty cut.

Ending, restating the beginning:

> They claim that it would create jobs, reduce inflation and eliminate the sky-rocketing costs of fighting the bootleggers.
>
> 'The case for a reduction is overwhelming,' says Anthony Fuller. No it isn't, says the Government.
>
> While they argue our pubs die. And only the bootleggers prosper.
> *Sun*

Tightly written at 850 words and mercifully free of 'Lottery love rat' cliché.

Next a column, essentially a think-piece, by an accomplished writer whose subject each week is office life. Because he has a devoted following, he can start with a simple statement then move gently and by understatement into overstatement, contrasting 'motivationally challenged' with the much more effective alternative description.

> In business these days, we are all encouraged to work smarter, not harder. This ignores the fact that there is a hardcore of people who don't work smart or hard; in fact, they hardly work at all. They are the 'motivationally challenged' – traditionally known as lazy sods – and every office has at least one of them.

He then moves into a form of context par, setting out the situation with an explanation that might have eluded the busy.

> Strangely, lazy sods are always the busiest people in the office. Whenever you ask them to do anything, there is no way they can help because they are far, far too busy. If you ever get irritated and ask them exactly what it is that they're so busy doing, they will have a long list of things that sound devilishly important. The truth is, if you'd asked them the same question a year earlier, the list of things would have been exactly the same.

At this point, as with most funny columns, the writer has to move into hyperbole, but exaggeration based on truth.

> Lazy people actually lead very full lives because they take an arse-achingly long time to do simple things such as photocopying. . . .

The subject is now examined from a number of angles: lazy sods at meetings (happy because they don't have to do any work) followed by how to get lazy sods to do any work (impossible – do it yourself). The conclusion looks at the place of lazy sods in any organisation.

> You would have thought that lazy people would form an inert mass at the bottom of an organisation. On the contrary, they are found at all levels in business, right up to chairman. The reason for this is simple: when something goes wrong in business, it's generally because someone somewhere has tried to do something. Obviously, if you don't do anything, you can't be blamed when it goes wrong. People who sit all day . . . busily straightening paperclips, are therefore the only people with a 100 per cent record of success. And with that sort of record, the world is their oyster.
> Guy Browning, *Guardian* Weekend magazine

Features involving a one-person interview are among the simpler to structure. This ghosted feature starts with memories of an armed robbery.

> Blink. He is wearing a black polo-neck and a black mask with slits for eyes. The end of a double-barrelled shotgun is inches from my eyes. He knows as well as I do that the glass between us isn't bullet-proof. My life doesn't flash before me but I see a clear picture of my daughter being told her mum is dead. That's all I can think of. Blink.

Context par:

> Every time I blinked that is what I saw. The flashbacks were horribly vivid. When a stranger points a shotgun at your face they're in control and you are left floundering. I floundered for two-and-a-half years. Every day I lost more control, and when I slept my dreams were full of monsters.

Start of main body copy. First section, re-telling the event.

> It was just after 10am on a December day in 1992 at a sub-branch of Barclays in Leeds where I worked behind the cash desk. There had been two attempted robberies in the past two months and both times I was shocked but seemed to recover. . . .
>
> The third time was different. . . .

Second section: the consequences with specific details.

> After the robbery I developed this irrational fear that the robbers would come back and get me. I started having nightmares in the form of flashbacks – but it was not only when I slept. It could be just when I closed my eyes.
>
> I became very remote and territorial . . . I stopped showing any emotions to my family. I reasoned that if they didn't love me as much they wouldn't miss me when I was killed. . . .

Third section: hope dawns.

> After two-and-half years a friend told me about a program at Long Lartin prison in the Vale of Evesham where psychologists were bringing victims into contact with perpetrators. . . .
>
> Walking into Long Lartin was a pivotal moment in my life. I was expecting the armed robbers there to be the evil monsters of my nightmares, but they weren't. . . . When the day ended I felt relief. I went home and slept and have never had trouble sleeping since. . . .

Working up to the conclusion: surprise, this isn't another first-person 'TOTTY' (Triumph over Tragedy).

> I am lucky because Barclays has seconded me to my current post – working in prisons making criminals consider the human cost of their violence – and has agreed to pay my salary for a year.

Conclusion: the writer's attitude has changed.

> I still get emotional, even though the nightmares have gone. It was an event that changed my life and the way I think about criminals. I used to be a bang-them-up-with-bread-and-water person, now I believe in rehabilitation. I've never met the men who robbed my branch, but I know where they are and the sentences they are serving. I'll never forgive them, but I meet so many armed robbers that they've just become two of many.
> *Big Issue*

Learning to structure isn't easy but it is worth all the effort.

ENDINGS

Readers who find a feature's first par mildly interesting often sample the end before deciding whether to read the rest, so the last par grows in importance. A well-crafted ending rewards both the hooked and the 'dip in' reader by offering a satisfying conclusion, nailing the feature down firmly. Don't fall into the essay or speech trap by repeating the intro.

Features often end with statements or quotes; less commonly with anecdotes and descriptions; rarely with questions. Whatever the style chosen, it should suit the feature, reader and publication. Concluding statements, for example, can be positive, negative, tentative even. They can hammer or thump home a point. What they should avoid is being timid or apologetic, slinking away out of sight.

Often the most effective conclusions echo the start but show the reader how much progress has been achieved or how much ground has been covered. Probably more than anywhere else in a feature, knowledge of the power points in a sentence pays off. The most forceful endings put the most important word at the end, in the final 'punch' position.

The Michael Parkinson interview quoted on page 57, for example, begins with an anecdote from a previous encounter, with Parkinson 'maybe slightly squiffy . . . the most famous person at the table'. It ends with a quote from the interview.

> But still he's jittery enough for one subject to be off-limits. What about his football team Barnsley, which has made it to the Premier League? 'Oh well, I mean, I don't wish to talk about this actually,' he says, suddenly bashful. Why not? 'Because the problem is that Barnsley might be relegated . . . and I don't want to go down the same chute.'

A conclusion that shows a sea-change, contrasting vividly with the intro, and allows readers to draw their own conclusions.

A feature starting:

> My first instinct was that Judy Hall was barking mad. My second was that I would be, too, if I didn't get out of there as quickly as possible.

ends:

> I don't know, but as I drove away across the Wiltshire Downs I felt lighter and less sceptical than I had been four hours earlier. A ghost had been laid to rest.
> Annabel Heseltine, *Daily Mail*

This time it's a positive contrast. The writer, who wanted to get out as quickly as possible in the intro, stayed for four hours and left with changed perceptions.

Endings often work best when they embody some conclusion reached during the research: in effect, an informed overview that aims to benefit the reader.

The first par of the *Sunday Telegraph* political analysis feature on page 55 ended:

> . . . the life and soul of the new Conservative Party, and the bedrock of its support, is Essex man.

This was Essex Man's first outing, before he'd acquired his second capital letter. Readers not sufficiently convinced of the importance of reading on, suspicious that EM might be a concept dreamed up by an inventive hack, might have looked at the end of the feature:

> . . . Essex man . . . is in the vanguard now: and however much he may offend those who wield the power he gives them, he will be in the vanguard for some time to come.

The intro to a feature on libel lawyers starts with an analogy that all but the smuggest swot can identify with.

> Watching your editor read a solicitor's letter threatening libel is like watching your parents read your school report. You may have goofed, but don't panic – unless the letter is from [five law firms mentioned].

It ends:

> If more publishers had a bit of guts, a lot of these threatening letters could be stopped dead.
> *Journalist's Week*

The feature included the information that there were (then) a total of possibly 100 lawyers expert in libel law and that almost all solicitors' letters were uninformed posturing. Reassuring and helpful.

Here's the conclusion to the intro on page 60 about staff appraisal, in a magazine designed for busy top-level accountants.

> Appraisal systems are the last ditch attempt by personnel to get managers to do some (people) managing. The problem is that they

give managers an excuse not to do it the rest of the year. The answer is not to spend money and time on useless systems but to insist that managers manage – and that they are willing, able and motivated to give objective, timely and helpful feedback to their staff appropriate to their level of readiness. Spend the personnel manager's time on reinforcing this, not on collecting bits of paper.
Accountancy

This ending could achieve Level 4 on the feature scale (see page 50) and produce positive action.

A *Cosmopolitan* feature begins:

On the face of it, Cedric is not an attractive man. For example, I was talking to him last night when he jumped up, shouted 'slugs' and ran out into the garden. He cuts them in half with a pair of scissors. This obsession makes the slugs and everybody else very nervous.

Don't think, though, that Cedric doesn't have his moments with women. Some of them (women) actually like him or – to be more accurate – are drawn to one of the 38 different people who reside inside Cedric's soul.

It ends:

It's strange the effect that some human beings have on others. Some people can bring out all the goodness within us, all the love, all the magic, and it's very beautiful when it happens. I wish it would happen more often. It's up to you, and to me, to see that it does. In the garden of love there is a flower called vulnerability. Of that much I am sure.

This is an example of pop psychology writing at its best: not prescriptive but persuasive.

Good quotes sit easily at the end of a feature, particularly a profile. As before, though, they need to be good.

Here's the ending of the feature (page 59) on the Tham Krabok de-tox programme run by Buddhist monks. It becomes clear they are unwilling to export their expertise. A monk talking:

They started a programme in Atlanta, Georgia, in the United States and, so it's said, seven people died of heart failure on the seventh day. I'm sorry, but only at Tham Krabok will it happen.

Now the reader knows why. Gruesome to the end.

EXTRAS

Boxes, panels and sidebars may look like afterthoughts but they're now integral to features. Almost every writer needs to think about them, if not at the idea stage then during research.

Content and style are determined by readers' interests and the time they have to spare. Writing should be concise, telegrammatic even. Easy reading is the key: short subject–verb–object sentences. Even subject–object phrases. Clauses should be kept to a minimum.

Besides being used to convey facts digestibly and encapsulate advice, they can make quite sophisticated points purely by positioning.

Journalists often give PRs a hard time, bludgeoning them for immediate help and offering scant thanks. Here's where courtesy and consideration pay off, as PRs are able to do much of the labour-intensive work, providing information for extras that might otherwise take lengthy dredging.

Simple facts: box

Concluding a feature on a children's book centre:

> Norfolk Children's Book Centre, Alby, Norwich, Norfolk NR11 7HB.
> Tel: 01263 768167.
> E-mail: ncbc@argonet.co.uk.
> Web site: http://www.argonet.co.uk/ncbc
> Open 10am–4pm and at other times to teachers by appointment.
> Closed Sundays and bank holidays.
> *Times Education Supplement*

Lots of relevant information, clearly punctuated. After accuracy, the most important thing to remember in boxes is intelligent punctuation. 'Opening times 10am–noon, 2pm–4pm Monday–Tuesday, early closing Wednesday 10am–noon, Saturdays 9am–4pm . . . ' Any more of that and readers will be lost. Here's where full stops, dashes and semicolons prove their worth.

Complex facts: table

An *Independent on Sunday* feature on Margaret Thatcher's cabinet shuffles between 1979 and 1990 used a table showing every post and holder in her

15 cabinets. Simple lists would have included the same information but would not have shown so clearly cabinet upward and downward mobility, promotions or relegations.

Large quantities of information: boxes and pars

A *Horse* magazine interview with owners of a livery stable, three of whose horses died after eating acorns, had five 'extras':

- fact box on the likelihood of horses dying from eating poisonous plants, including preventive action owners could take
- illustrated panels of 14 mildly toxic, toxic and fatal plants (see *Yew* below)
- fact box on ragwort, the commonest cause of poisoning; where to obtain free information
- small par offering free information on revitalising grazing from a specialist organisation
- small par on the forthcoming second edition of book on equine nutrition and feeding.

> Yew
> Appearance: Evergreen shrub or small tree, reaching 20m and living for up to 1,500 years. Reddish bark, dark needle-like leaves, small yellow bead-like (male) or green pear-shaped (female) flowers in March and bright red hollow-ended berries in late September.
> Habitat: Parks, churchyards, broad-leaved woods and chalk downlands.
> Effect: Muscle tremors, incoordination, nervousness, difficulty in breathing, diarrhoea, convulsions, collapse and heart failure.
> Toxin: Taxine, a potent alkaloid.
> HORSE WARNING: A horse eating as little as 0.05% of his bodyweight will prove fatal.

OK, the author enlisted expert help and didn't write all the extras herself but she did the thinking and planning, customising the valuable practical information for the 90 per cent plus female, horse-mad readership. That 'HORSE WARNING' is a sure sign of focused thinking (though wobbly sentence construction).

Encapsulated information boxes

AVIATION MODELLER INTERNATIONAL
Who reads it. Men who have an unnatural obsession with balsa wood.
Most worrying bit. Shane Harding, whose home-made 'fun-fly' aeroplane is named Groin Strain.
Most informative bit. 'Pat McCaulay discusses his techniques for cutting accurate wing cores.'
Saddest bit. 'When I was young I was deprived. I never had a Kalper micro-diesel engine.' It's like *Fever Pitch* all over again, isn't it?
Any interest for women? The only women here are in the ads, holding up Hawker Typhoons with a winsome smile.
B magazine guide to male-interest magazines

Added-value boxes

Some specialist magazines use extras from other writers to widen the scope of a feature. Added to Jeff Dawson's *Empire* interview with Harrison Ford, tied to the release of the movie *Air Force One*, was:

*   box describing five other movies featuring terrorists
*   fanciful pix and caption box: 'What if other movie stars fancied running for President?'
*   fact box on the US President's planes:

    Air Force One is not a plane, but a call sign. The President has two planes at his disposal, both Boeing 747–200Bs, and whichever one is in the sky is Air Force One. . . .

    Each one can carry 102 people including the 26 crew it takes to fly and run the thing. . . .

    There are six khazis on board plus a special one for the Prez. And facilities for the handicapped.

Speed-read summary boxes

Despite having highly educated readers in terms of years spent studying, doctors' magazines often have features with bullet-point boxes in large type which repeat the main findings boiled down to a few sentences. These are the journalistic equivalent of 'executive summary' pars designed for hyper-busy readers.

Key points
- Conservative therapy in the form of physiotherapy by an experienced and interested physiotherapist is the first-line management of GSI
- Burch colposuspension can give an 90 per cent objective cure rate and is the current 'gold standard' surgical treatment for GSI
- Continence devices may be useful in the short-term in women awaiting surgery or in the longer-term in those not suitable for or who do not wish to undergo surgery
- Newer surgical techniques may offer less invasive treatment but careful appraisal is needed before they are adopted universally

Pulse

Statistics

The best way to make stats readable is to delete verbs, adjectives, adverbs and pronouns and put what remains under relevant headings.

Autocar's 'Performance and Specifications' boxes detail the featured car's

- engine layout
- max power
- max torque
- specific output
- power to weight
- torque to weight
- installation
- construction
- bore/stroke
- valve gear
- compression ratio
- ignition
- fuel.

That's just the engine. Other sections include gearbox, suspension, acceleration and on and on. Not a verb or adjective anywhere.

Advice boxes

Amateur Photographer's '8 lenses to die for' product round-up included: an intro/overview of add-on lenses for single-lens reflex cameras; reviews of the eight lenses; and, for extras, two advice boxes: 'Downsize your format' and 'Five top lenses usage tips'. Example:

Never underestimate the amount of camera shake that your unsupported body will create. Always support your lens and camera when the shutter speed drops below a safe handholdable level. . . .

If you want candid shots with a wide-angle lens, set your aperture to f/11 at 2m and shoot without focusing . . .

Sidebars to make a point

Decorating a feature on Jonathan Aitken after his 'cancer of bent and twisted journalism' speech, was a simple sidebar alongside his picture:

> NUJ CODE OF CONDUCT – CLAUSE 2
> A journalist shall at all times defend the principle of the freedom of the press and other media in relation to the collection of information and expression of comment and criticism. He/she shall strive to eliminate distortion, news suppression and censorship.
> *Journalist*

Point made.

THREE FEATURES

The features that follow are not flawlessly crafted exhibits from the Museum of the Written Word, reverently preserved under glass in subdued lighting. They're here because they work: the writing flows, the details are graphic and the words are well chosen.

News feature (daily paper)

ABBEY OVERFLOWS FOR COMPTON

Matthew Engel attends a service to celebrate the cricketer whose innings has left an indelible imprint.

He was not royalty (not as such). He was not a great statesman (his politics were a touch, well, simplistic). He was not a candidate for Poets' Corner (judging from his contributions to the Sunday Express). He was not holy.

And yet Westminster Abbey was filled to overflowing yesterday to mark the passing of Denis Compton. Two thousand people turned up; a thousand had their applications rejected, the abbey's biggest case of over-subscription for a memorial service since Richard Dimbleby died in 1966.

Dimbleby died at the height of his broadcasting fame. Compton died on April 23, aged 78. No one under 50 can even have any memory of seeing him do what he did best: play cricket sublimely, and with an air that the whole thing was the most ridiculous lark.

And you would have to be pushing 60 to remember his apotheosis, the summer of 1947. Exactly 50 years ago this week, when an Old Trafford Test was on, just as it will be tomorrow, Compton scored 115 for England against South Africa, an innings described by Wisden as 'delightful and impudent'.

That was just one of the 18 centuries he scored that extraordinary summer, when Britain at last began to feel the war was over. Compton was the embodiment of that feeling. And thus when the Dean of Westminster said that we had gathered to give thanks for the life of Denis Compton, it did not feel like a clergyman's phrase, but the literal truth. We were not just remembering someone who happened to be amazingly successful (the idea of a man good enough to play both football and cricket for England is now unthinkable), we were honouring someone who made an indelible imprint on the life of the nation.

Among the 2,000 were many you would have expected: dozens of retired cricketers, one former prime minister (no prizes) and all the showbizzy Taverner-types with whom Compton mixed so easily.

But there were hundreds of unknown folk, too, and some highly improbable ones – like Dennis Skinner who was on his way to the Commons, asked what the fuss was, and was ushered in as a special guest.

Skinner watched Compton play at Derby. 'I expect we were miles apart politically. But he was an adventurer, wasn't he? He took risks. He was everything that Boycott wasn't.'

The ceremony itself was fairly standard issue: I Vow To Thee My Country, Jerusalem and Pomp and Circumstance to finish, but all beautifully done. The chairman of Arsenal read Let us Now Praise Famous Men; E W Swanton, still thunderous at 90, read Cardus on Lord's.

The address was given by Compton's one-time Middlesex team-mate and long-standing buddy, J J Warr, who delved briefly into the treasure chest of Compton-iana. These tales mostly rely on Compo's famously casual attitude to everything.

'In May 1967 he announced he was going to have an enormous party for his 50th birthday. His mother phoned him and said: "It's a good idea, Denis, but you're only 49." It was one of the few occasions when he was early for anything.'

One did half-expect Compo to wander in at any moment, late and full of apologies. It could have been the young daredevil of 1947 or the old man – knee and hips crocked – leaning on his stick. He had star quality throughout his life, which is what brought us to the abbey.

The decision to stage the Compton ceremony, made by the Dean, Wesley Carr, appears to be part of a trend towards populism in abbey memorial services. Brian Johnston, Les Dawson and Bobby Moore have recently received this very final British accolade. In contrast, politicians are now usually dealt with at St Margaret's, Westminster.

The honour would not have bothered Compo that much. As Warr said, his CBE was last seen hanging round the neck of his Old English sheepdog. But he would have loved the occasion, and the chance for a last drink with his very special chums. All 2,000 of them.
Guardian, July 2 1997

This is rich writing, covering a news event and adding so much more in background colour and detail. At the end readers have the sense of having been at the service. They know the hymns, the readings, who spoke the eulogy. 'We were there,' says Engel editorialising in a very un-newsy way, witness those rather intrusive early brackets.

Readers learn a great detail about Compton, his cricket (particular score on a particular date on a particular ground and the number of centuries scored in a particular year), his character and lifestyle, his sporting abilities, his friends and admirers – and also about Britain in 1947. Also, details of the most heavily subscribed memorial services at Westminster Abbey, names of recent celebrities honoured, the location for many politicians' memorial services, and on and on. Even two visual images of Compton young and old. And it's all wrapped up with a conclusion including an affectionate anecdote, the 1940-ish word 'chums' and a feeling of the Abbey packed with friends and admirers paying tribute to a remarkable man.

The structure is not the usual sequential approach, but proceeds at first by negatives, builds up his reputation using figures and contrast with the Richard Dimbleby memorial service, describes his career, starts on the ceremony, describes those present including a quote from a surprise attender, gives more details of the ceremony, then covers the address, goes back to other services and ends with an anecdote and an affectionate wrap. And it all flows smoothly with the genesis of each par discernible in the previous one.

Trade feature (weekly)

PICNIC IN THE BEDROOM

James Thomas, 36, joined London's Dorset Square Hotel as general manager in November 1996. 'Bedroom picnics' are the latest innovation he has dreamt up in his quest to provide home-from-home service.

Two or three mornings a week, I wake up in the hotel. If I've worked late the night before, I might decide to forgo a battle with the Underground and grab a spare room. As well as being convenient, this gives me a chance to see how the hotel operates from a customer's point of view.

If I have stayed overnight, I'll enjoy the luxury of eggs and bacon – and I'll always taste the coffee and pastries to check the quality of our supplies.

🕐 If I've come in from home, I'll get in between 8 and 9am. The first thing I'll do is read the night manager's book and check up on the overnight occupancy and room rates.

My morning will be spent around reception, chatting to guests, opening mail and speaking to maintenance and housekeeping. This is a small hotel – only 38 bedrooms – so my job as general manager is very much hands-on. We're all multi-faceted here. For instance, we don't have a personnel or training manager, so my job encompasses both those roles.

🕐 Every Tuesday morning at 11am, I meet with the other hotel general managers in the Firmdale group at the company's head office in South Kensington. There are just five of us, all managing small luxury hotels in London. The others are women, which is great because they're so chatty. I know that's a sexist thing to say, but I have to be sexist because I'm the underdog.

At lunchtime I'll spend some time in the kitchen watching the service. I'll then nip out for a sandwich from the deli on the corner. I could get something to eat in the hotel but it's important to get off the premises just for 20 minutes, especially if I've stayed in the hotel the previous night.

It's also necessary to observe what's going on in the local area. For instance, by going out of the hotel, we discovered that many of our US guests were skipping breakfast in the hotel and grabbing a bagel from the deli before jumping into a taxi en route to their meetings. So we've now introduced 'Breakfast to go'. Five minutes after ordering it, guests can pick up a Dorset Square Hotel paper bag – containing juice, coffee and a pastry – from reception as they go out the door.

🕝 About 2.30pm I disappear into my broom cupboard of an office to get on with some paperwork. This is also a chance to develop new ideas. It's important to be creative. You can't afford to stand still – it's good for business and it stops the staff getting bored.

My latest project is 'Bedroom picnics', a name that we're going to trademark. The idea stems from last summer, when I returned from the theatre one night with a girlfriend and we felt a bit peckish, but weren't sure what we wanted to eat. Our head chef, Trevor Baines, said he would put together a few nibbly bits. It was great – a selection of all the kinds of things you like to eat in a relaxed way.

We've now developed the idea for room service. It is served on a large wicker tray with a green gingham cloth – perfect for putting on the bed to eat while watching the television, planning your next day's meeting, running the bath – or even in the bath. We wanted to get away from formal room service and provide something that guests can pick at with their fingers in the relaxed setting of their room.

The contents must be simple enough to be put together in a few minutes, even by the night porter. A typical picnic would include vegetable crudities and a dip, a selection of cold meat such as salami, Parma ham and turkey, hot Toulouse sausages with an onion and mustard dip, prawns in filo pastry, smoked salmon, cheese, bread and freshly sliced fruit.

I am just as likely to deliver the Bedroom picnic to a guest's room myself as is one of the restaurant staff.

🕕 At about 6pm I write personal arrival notes to all the guests, which are delivered at turn-down. We know every guest's name and what kind of business they're in. Every Thursday evening between 6 and 7pm, all guests are invited for cocktails in the restaurant.

🕗 I'll eat dinner in the hotel restaurant – the Potting Shed – two or three times a week. If not, I leave the hotel between 8 and 9pm. By then most of the arrivals are in, the turn-downs are done and the

restaurant is buzzing. Going home to Docklands is a great antidote
to all this – I read or watch TV.

Janet Harmer, *Caterer and Hotelkeeper*, 11 June 1998

Reproduced with the permission of the editor of *Caterer and Hotelkeeper*.

The feature was accompanied by a Factfile on the hotel, including address, telephone numbers, owner, number of bedrooms and room rates.

This is a variation on the *Sunday Times* 'Life in the Day of' page. The feature profiles a catering personality by describing a typical working day which exemplifies many. It includes a great deal of valuable hotel information: staffing attitudes, how often figures are checked, managers' meetings, how ideas to generate extra breakfast income are developed, a new idea copyable – under a different name – and how to run it, guest pampering, etc. The writing is deceptively simple, mostly in the present tense and requires no links except the use of the time. The style fits the catering and hotel business: hard-working, gossipy, people-oriented and rather like show business with its search for the new. By the end, the reader has a very good idea of the hotel and its general manager, together with some new ideas to ponder and maybe adapt.

Feature requiring detailed research (glossy monthly)

I LOVE THE JOB, BUT DO I HAVE TO WEAR THAT HAT?

Uniforms have come a long way since the nylon overall – or have they? Getting your corporate kit on can provoke mixed feelings, as Kerry Fowler discovers.

There's something about a woman in uniform, whether she's selling a low-rate mortgage or serving a G&T at 30,000 feet. When they're right, the clothes inspire confidence: trust me, they say. When they're wrong, the company looks tacky and the trendiest woman feels frumpy, no matter how hard she tries. As Leonie Barrie, Editor of *Company Clothing* magazine (the industry's style bible), says, 'It's a very emotive subject. People who have to wear uniforms are acutely aware of others' reactions.'

Uniforms flash up all sorts of message – fear (ticket collectors and traffic wardens), respect (look how far Deirdre's 'airline pilot' in *Coronation Street* fell from grace when it turned out he was just a silk-tie hawker) and instant recognition of who's staff and who isn't ('Ask the man in the hat, he'll know'). 'A uniform signals competence, kindliness and a host of other skills much more dramatically than the way you sit or stand, or the expression on your face,' says Halla Beloff, social psychologist at Edinburgh University.

Granted, if you have to wear a Mrs Overall pinny your expression may not have the same radiance as the girl at the Dior counter, but at least these practical numbers keep clothes clean. Better still, they simplify life. GH nutritionist Fiona Hunter is wistful about the white cotton dress she wore as a hospital dietician. 'I had 15 minutes extra in bed,' she says. 'I didn't have to think about what to wear. I didn't have to spend money on work clothes and it was all laundered for me. Now I have a clothes crisis every morning.'

But isn't that preferable to getting kitted up to look like Nell Gwyn? Not according to the supervisor at the Beefeater By the Tower (of London) restaurant. 'Dressing up is all part of the job,' she says. 'Sometimes the girls don't like the mob caps, but otherwise they enjoy it.' And what of the message conveyed by their wench-type costumes? Surprisingly, she's never had a problem in all her 23 years there. 'The outfits are quite demure and the maids have to wear discreet white bras under the camisole. We do get the occasional enquiry as to whether we're a topless restaurant but, that aside, we don't really tend to get rude comments,' she says.

Confusion is much more likely at London's trendy Pharmacy restaurant (part-owned by Damien Hirst), where the receptionists wear Prada-designed doctors' coats and the waiters have surgeons' jackets. Are they there to give you a good time or serve up a prognosis you wonder.

No such mystery surrounds the tartan army at Caledonian Airways, who thrive on the attention their kilts and frilly jabots bring. 'Americans are wild about them,' says purser Jill Mellor. 'We get stopped on concourses all round the world by people wanting to know who we work for.' A hefty staff manual details everything from the position of the kilt pin to the tilt of the tam-o'-shanter.

'The quality of the outfit shows workers the kind of respect paid by the employer,' says Halla Beloff. 'What they wear has to inspire confidence. It has to be clean and decent, but it should also be up to date and it certainly shouldn't be bizarre. A bad uniform can put you in a bad mood and you need to feel good if you're interacting with people.'

Elizabeth, now a dance teacher, is still spooked by her experience in a Sainsbury's uniform 10 years ago. 'I can't express how much I hated wearing it,' she says. 'I looked like a bell – a big orange and brown nylon bell. But,' she adds, 'I did meet my husband while I was on the checkout . . . '

These days, many companies turn to fashion designers for help.

Sainsbury's has signed up Paul Costelloe, who revamped BA; John Rocha designs for Virgin Airlines; Bruce Oldfield has put together a range of workwear for everyone from nurses to chefs; and Jeff Banks has left his mark on Asda, Barclays Bank, Iceland and many more. 'It's a major status symbol,' says Jeff. 'Organisations spend a lot on graphics and literature and finally the penny drops: if you want to make a company buzz, make sure the staff are happy with the way they look.' Designers can't afford any catwalk precious-ness, though. 'They're not just catering for size 8–18s, it's more like 6–40s,' says Leonie Barrie. 'They've also got to think about ethnic designs and maternity wear.'

So what's the secret of creating a classy livery? 'There's a reason why I say wardrobe and not uniform,' says Jeff, who estimates around 500,000 people spend the day in his corporate designs. 'The wardrobe I did for Barclays has a printed "flippy" skirt and shaped blouse that would suit an 18-year-old and a looser over-shirt, pleated skirt and loose striped jacket that would be fine for a 55-year-old woman. (If you're over 50 and still feeling flippy, the choice of skirts is up to you.) But they still look as if they play for the same team.'

You can be a team-player even if you're not in front of house, and most occupations have an unwritten dress code – pin-stripes for accountants, chinos for computer buffs, Armani for media moguls. Sometimes it's more prescriptive: at John Lewis, while the 'partners' (as the rank and file are known) wear navy and green outfits, the section managers select from Jaeger or Country Casuals, and choose from black and blue, too. It's like the old sixth-form privilege: instead of a boater you get to wear a skull cap.

London barrister Barbara Hewson conforms to a dress code devised over 200 years ago: 'Nothing much has changed except the price – the horsehair wig now costs around £340.' For fledgling legal eagles, though, it can be worth the outlay. 'Your client immediately knows who you are when you're in your kit,' she says.

The perverse psychology is that none of us wants to be a clone. Schoolgirls aren't the only ones to customise their uniforms. The Britannia stewardesses in the TV documentary *Airline* are asked to wear red lipstick to match their corporate scarf but, apparently, some slide down the spectrum until they hit pink. We all, it seems, like to be unique beneath the serge.

Good Housekeeping, June 1998

A lot of research went into this feature – 19 firms or types of business are mentioned and seven people are quoted – yet the whole flows smoothly. The writing is full of images, which is as it should be since the subject is visual. The lively quotes give insight into the subject.

The range of uniforms covered is impressively wide: from airlines to supermarkets, theme restaurants to posh eateries, barristers to schoolgirls. The quotes read well and are in different voices, suggesting that the writer can probably do shorthand and doesn't recast everything into her own style.

There's a deft touch with words: 'radiance' is used as a semi-sendup for a girl at the Dior counter, contrasting with 'tacky' and 'frumpy' elsewhere; the nutritionist is 'wistful' about the pluses of her old uniformed life. There's evidence of practical thinking and questioning: the sizes that are catered for, for example, and different styles for different age and size groups.

The piece runs smoothly because of deft linking and by the end the reader has been entertained, informed and enlightened.

4
Writing reviews
Harriett Gilbert

WHAT IS A REVIEW?

> The new Tarantino? Well, it's not *bad*. The acting's pretty terrific, especially that Seventies blaxploitation star . . . what's her name? Pam Grier. But in the end it's rather . . . slow and steady, you know? Rather ponderous.

What you have just read is a review: in other words, a critical assessment of an art form or an entertainment. You have probably been speaking reviews since you first saw a movie or went to a restaurant.

A 'listing' is different. It need do nothing more than provide the reader or listener with factual information:

> 10.50: The Jack Docherty Show: with Douglas Adams

A review, as well as providing that kind of information, should describe the work and express an opinion about it.

WHAT DOES IT TAKE TO BE A REVIEWER?

This raises a fundamental question. Although everyone has a right to express their opinion, why should certain opinions have the privilege of being published? Why should a small group of journalists be allowed to discourage strangers from buying a book they might otherwise have read, or to urge them to spend their money on expensive concert tickets?

One part of the answer is that they perform a service. With so much art and entertainment to choose from, critical sifting is vital. Another is that a good reviewer accepts that the privilege of influencing strangers carries responsibilities.

'I never read a book before reviewing it – it prejudices a man so.'
Sydney Smith

The first is to know what you are talking about. You should, at least, have seen, eaten at, listened to or read the thing you are reviewing. It is not enough (as occasionally happens) to rewrite or even copy a publicist's blurb.

'A critic is a bunch of biases held loosely together by a sense of taste.'
Witney Balliett

You should also know what you like, what you hate, and why. If, for instance, you find that all television programmes are much of a muchness, think again before pursuing a career as a television critic. This does not mean that your tastes should be set in cement (indeed, it would be extremely odd if they stayed the same throughout your life); it simply means you should care.

There are some who argue that, more than that, you should be an expert in your field. There is much to be said for expertise – and, if you want to make reviewing the central plank of your career, you should undoubtedly work to acquire expertise in your chosen area – but a useful review may still be written by a thoughtful beginner or occasional reviewer.

In fact, a beginner or occasional reviewer can sometimes have the edge. As A A Gill has said about his job as a restaurant critic:

> In most jobs experience is a boon, but for a critic it puts an ever-lengthening distance between you and your reader. The vast majority of diners don't eat with knowledge, they eat with friends. They don't know what happens on the other side of the swing door. Why should they? Most people eat out rarely and with high expectations, not every day with a knowing smirk.

'One always tends to overpraise a long book because one has got through it.'
E M Forster

All reviewers should be aware that experience and knowledge remove them from their readers. For instance, because they experience so much that is bad – stuff from which they protect the public with their subsequent panning reviews – they should recognise that sometimes, in gratitude, they see the merely good as being brilliant. And their physical encounter with the things they review is rarely the same as the punters'. On the one hand, they usually have the best theatre seats, and can visit art shows before the public surges in to obscure the exhibits. Often, too, they receive advance tapes of television and radio programmes to watch or listen to whenever convenient. On the other hand, they may be summoned to *group* television previews, in preview theatres not obviously designed to resemble comfortable sitting rooms, and critics usually watch films in the morning, in cinemas empty except for them and a half-awake scattering of their colleagues. A good reviewer should bear these abnormalities in mind.

'Critics are like eunuchs in a harem: they know how it's done, they've seen it done every day, but they're unable to do it themselves.'
Brendan Behan

Some artists find it objectionable for their work to be reviewed by non-practitioners. Book critics are, at least, writers. Some of them have even written books. But many reviewers of film, theatre, art, dance, music, and so on, have never actually practised the form, however great their theoretical knowledge.

Painters frequently grumble about their work being judged by 'art historians' (the scorn with which they utter those words would lead you to suppose they were talking of vampires). Theatre people are even more vociferous – for two reasons.

The first is purely economic. Every performance of a play is expensive, what with wages, lighting, rental of the theatre, and so on. So, if the first-night reviews are hostile, companies cannot afford to continue performing to empty or half-empty houses, hoping that audiences will gradually be drawn by word of mouth. The second reason is that theatre is *immediate*. Film-makers, writers and painters, in contrast, have long ago finished creating their work by the time the reviews appear. And, although of course they suffer whenever their work is damned, the process is even more painful for those who must read of their failures and inadequacies when, in effect, they are still in the process of creating.

And drama critics can have an extraordinary influence. So great was the power of the New York critic Clive Barnes that Broadway managements are said to have scoured the telephone directories for other Clive Barneses, invited them along to opening nights and pasted their praise – 'The best play I've seen: Clive Barnes' – on the flanks of their theatres.

But still: does this mean that reviewers should also be practitioners? Many in the British theatre think so and, in order to prove their point, they once challenged the drama critics to try directing a play. A few accepted, including the notoriously scathing Nicholas de Jongh of the London *Evening Standard*. The resultant productions were widely agreed to be worthy at best, terrible at worst. While this may have gratified the challengers, however, it proved only that good reviewers are *not* necessarily good practitioners.

It is important to understand the limitations and potential of an art form – to recognise, for instance, that a play can do things that a film cannot, and vice versa – but it is not essential to be able to practise it yourself.

'Asking a working writer what he feels about critics is like asking a lamp-post what it feels about dogs.'
    John Osborne

If the anger of theatre people is caused, in part, by the devastating power of bad reviews, it is also caused by a widespread belief (among artists) that the primary role of reviewers is to nurture and promote the form about which they write.

It certainly is an important role. Obscure bands; avant-garde artists; authors attempting new forms of fiction: without the encouragement and publicity provided by sympathetic reviewers, these would have an even harder time than they do gaining recognition. Art critics such as *Time Out*'s Sarah Kent helped to promote and explain the New British Artists. The theatre critic Paul Allen (also, incidentally, a dramatist) has had a strong hand in ensuring that the BBC's coverage of theatre extends beyond London's West End. The marginalised, forgotten, unusual or difficult rely on critics to bring them to people's attention, to explain and to support them.

Well-established, commercial art forms are also helped by intelligent reviewing. Film critics such as Dilys Powell and Judith Williamson, for instance, have given their readers a deeper appreciation of popular cinema. But if critics did *nothing* but support and praise – or, indeed, nothing but carp and condemn – they would cease to have any impact. Their work would lose credibility and focus.

A paradox to be borne in mind is that readers frequently take their bearings from regular critics with whom they disagree but of whose preferences they are aware. If they know that a critic routinely dismisses or disparages something they enjoy, readers are perfectly capable of taking a thumbs-down as a thumbs-up. The clearer your views, the better you enable them to do this.

WRITE FOR YOUR READER

Centrally, critics must write for their readers, not for the artists whose work they are assessing (nor for fellow reviewers, however much they would like their good opinion). This does not mean that critics' opinions should twist and turn to make their readers happy; it means that critics should serve their readers. To do this, they must know who their readers are.

The readers of red-top tabloids, for instance, expect very few reviews – mainly previews of television programmes – but, what they get, they like to be short and snappy, followed as a rule by a 'star rating' (five stars for 'Don't miss it', one for 'Garbage', to quote the *Daily Star*). At the other end of the newspaper market, broadsheet readers are prepared for longer, more carefully argued reviews. A lead book review in the *Observer*, for example, might run to 1,000 words of description, argument and opinion. (Occasionally, reviews in the broadsheets never get to the opinion bit at all, especially reviews of biographies by writers who were acquainted with the subject and choose to devote their space to reminiscence. This is not an example to be followed.)

Some magazines – the *New Statesman*, for instance – also run single reviews at lengths of 900 or 1,000 words. But most magazines, from the cheapest weekly to the glossiest monthly, do not. This is partly because their designers refuse to have pages packed with grey columns of words. It is also because, when they do choose to run a lengthy piece on the arts, it is more likely to be in the form of a feature. So *Harpers & Queen* might run a 1,300-word feature on a novelist's life, but its lead book review will be 350 words, with subsidiary reviews (not only of books but also of movies or restaurants) often less than 100 words – much the same length as a record review in *Smash Hits*. Even *Time Out*, a magazine of which reviews are an important component, usually runs them at between 250 and 300 words, no more.

The time your readers expect to devote to reading your review is important, but length is far from being everything. Tone of voice matters, too. Readers of style magazines, for instance, or of magazines aimed at young people, tolerate endless injunctions about what is fashionable and what is not. This is from a review of the paperback reissue of Armistead Maupin's *Tales of the City* in *19* magazine:

> The first book in Maupin's six-volume Seventies saga, and as all
> things retro seem to be in (again!), a pretty trendy tome to be seen
> reading on the bus.

Readers of literary magazines, to take a different example, enjoy being
nudged by cultural references that it gives them satisfaction to recognise.

Understanding your readers' frame of reference is important. For
instance, writing for the *Daily Telegraph*, pop reviewer David Cheal can
use the phrase 'not with a bang but with a simper' confident that readers
will know the T S Eliot quote he has distorted. He would probably not do
the same were he reviewing for *Smash Hits*. Similarly, when writing for
the feminist magazine *Sibyl*, the literary critic Georgina Paul can talk of
the 'feminist reappropriation' of ancient Greek myth; her readers will
know what she means. But, were she writing for a local paper, the phrase
would need to be explained or (preferably) replaced.

Readers of local papers are perhaps the hardest to target. You know where
they live, and should take that into account when reviewing things
connected to the area, but, even more than with national papers, they
tend to differ widely in age, income, education, cultural interests and
politics. At least with most of the national press you know your readers'
probable politics and incomes.

Magazines are more narrowly focused. They may, overtly or otherwise,
be aimed at a particular sex or age group. There are magazines for people
with such and such a hobby, job, cultural interest, religion, political
affiliation. There are even magazines aimed at people of a particular
ethnic group or sexual orientation.

Their readers, of course, usually buy a whole range of publications. To take
just one example: a black British woman estate agent might regularly buy
the *Daily Mail*, the *Radio Times*, *Cosmopolitan* and *Pride*. Only in *Pride*, a
magazine specifically aimed at black readers, would she expect a review of
a gig by the Senegalese musician Cheikh Lo to open as Diana Evans's did:

> The Jazz Café is brimming with swaying 'world music' fans, most
> of whom, it has to be said, are white. It's the same with most
> concerts by African stars. The question arises, why is it that black
> people don't listen to their own music?

Whether your publication's readers are black people, schoolteachers, film
buffs, train spotters, gays, vegetarians, pensioners or clubbers, your review
should recognise that fact.

Once you have established who your readers are – their likely interests, frame of reference, verbal attention span, and so on – there are five further questions which, if you are to serve them well, you should ask yourself:

- Have I given the thing I'm reviewing my full, open-minded attention?
- Have I reached my assessment of it honestly: uninfluenced, for instance, by the fear of being out on a limb, the fear of upsetting the powerful, the temptation to be nasty for the fun of it, or the simple pleasure of kicking someone when they're up?
- Have I made my assessment clear?
- Have I provided my readers with enough descriptive and factual information for them to decide the value of my assessment?
- Is what I've written engaging – *to my particular readers?*

CELINE DION: *My Heart Will Go On.* Another slow smoocher from the Canadian diva, this is the love theme from the movie *Titanic.* Keep some stay-awake pills handy 'cos you might nod off during this one! It's not the most kickin' tune ever! She's got a great voice, but this song's a bit samey and boring.
Smash Hits

BULLY BEEF AND BURGHERS by James Callaway (published by the author at 54 Swain Street, Watchet, Somerset TA23). Railway preservationists may recall the author as a volunteer stationmaster at Abergynolwyn, on the Talyllyn Railway; he has now transferred to the broad gauge and is a supporter of the West Somerset Railway. This, his second book, is set on the British army-controlled railways of South Africa during the Boer War and concerns the military and amorous activities of Captain Robin Goodfellow, Royal Engineers, and his misadventures with an armoured train nicknamed 'Bully Beef'. It is a good-natured romp and greatly assisted your reviewer to survive a tedious train journey.
Railway Magazine

HOW TO RESEARCH

The amount of research you need do depends on three things. First is the ambitiousness of your review. A 1,000-word review of *Lolita* in which you intend to discuss the general issue of movie censorship will obviously need more preparatory reading than a straightforward 200-word review.

Second is the amount of information available. To review a Rolling Stones concert, for instance, you would need to become familiar not only with decades' worth of their work but with the accumulation of comment about it. The same would not be true for a concert by a new band.

Third, and in practice most important, is the amount of time you have. Specialist reviewers never stop researching, if only because their present work is a form of research for the future. Occasional reviewers must do what they can within the restraints of the deadline. And, although it is impossible to know too much, it is worth remembering that knowledge works best as a quiet foundation for what you write, not as rococo decoration splattered about all over the place. Its purpose is not to impress the readers with your brilliance, but to ensure the solidity and soundness of your judgement.

The most important element in research is examples of previous work (if any) by the artist or entertainer in question. These allow to you to spot recurrent themes, obsessions, strengths and weaknesses and to assess the relationship of the new work to the old. Also useful are press releases and cuttings from both the general and the specialist press. Reference books, too, are helpful (and, although they tend to be expensive, can often be found in libraries). For a list of a few that reviewers have found useful, see 'Reference for reviewers' in Further reading.

TAKE THE RIGHT NOTES

In most cases, you will have one chance to watch or listen to the work you are reviewing. Even with videos, CDs and books, although in theory you may flip back to the beginning as often as you like, in practice there may not be time for more than one go. So try to ensure that the notes you take are the right ones.

You need, first, to note those *facts* that you will need when you start to write: that the novel's narrator is a 60-year-old lawyer, for example; or that the opera has been relocated to 1930s Berlin.

Sense impressions are also important: the look of a stage set; the way the actor playing Hamlet uses his voice; the lighting of a rock concert; the dominant colours of a movie . . . whatever strikes you, make suffi-cient notes to be able to recreate it in print. And do keep *all* your senses alert. A film, for instance, is more than its narrative. It is also a complex of composition, lighting, movement and noise. As well as dialogue, the sound track will almost certainly have music on it, not to mention the sighing of wind or the constant throbbing of helicopter blades. The camera may cling to the actors' faces in close-up, or keep its distance.

Similarly, a dance performance consists not only of a sequence of movements more or less effectively performed, but also of music (or other sounds), lighting, costume and décor. Notice, *consciously* notice, all those things that are having an effect.

Quotes, where applicable, are also useful. Write down those that are powerful in themselves and those that could be used to make a wider point.

Finally, note your reactions. If you smile, cry, are frightened, are bored, put it down.

After all this, the next point to make is that you can take *too many* notes. Especially when reviewing a performance, if you spend all your time with your face in a notebook you are liable to miss key moments. So, be selective: note only those things that make a special impression.

Some critics make no notes at all until a performance is over, on the not unreasonable grounds that what they remember must be what most impressed them. If you trust your memory, try it. And, even if you have cautiously taken notes during the performance, it is still useful to write a quick sentence afterwards, to sum up your feelings: 'Pretentious rubbish; I couldn't understand a word of it', for instance, or 'Started slowly but, by the end, had me gripped'. The reason for this is to prevent you, later, from writing yourself towards an untruthful opinion. For various reasons, including doubts about your judgement, this is easy to do.

STRUCTURE

Magazines occasionally present reviews in a checklist format, as with this, from a column of identically structured album reviews in B magazine:

> **WHO** Carleen Anderson
> **WHAT** *Blessed Burden*
> **LISTEN TO IT** When you feel like being a funky diva. This woman has soul.
> **VERDICT**: Paul Weller produced most of it – that's how good it is. It took three years, but the result is a selection of the sweetest

tunes. Carleen, you've been gone way too long. **A delicious, delightful 7 out of 10**.

More often, you will need to build an appropriate framework for each review.

'Taking to pieces is the trade of those who cannot construct.'
Ralph Waldo Emerson

To build your framework, you should first remember that you cannot decide on the structure of any piece of journalism until you know what the story is – or, more precisely in the case of a review, whether you plan to give a thumbs-up, a thumbs-down or something in between. You also need to know why you have reached this verdict.

Take, for instance, this short review of Simple Minds' *Néapolis* album (published in the *Big Issue*):

> Once masters of stomping stadium rock, the Minds have become a watered-down version of atmospheric U2 pop circa the 'Zooropa' LP. Although there are charming touches such as 'War Babies', the likes of recent single 'Glitterball' will soon have you dozing off. Things improve with 'Androgyny', but when they finished recording the album in crime-ridden Naples (hence its title) any decent melodies they had must have been mugged and left for dead.

The reviewer, Gary Crossing, is giving the album a thumbs-down because, he believes, it demonstrates how musically *boring* Simple Minds have become. The structure of his review depends on this assessment. First, because he has few words to play with, he has ignored those aspects of the album irrelevant to his central point. This does not mean that he has suppressed the album's virtues; merely that he has put to one side those ingredients he considers peripheral: here, for example, the musicians' technical ability.

Second, to show the extent of his disappointment, he opens by reminding his readers that the band were once 'masters of stomping stadium rock'.

Then, what little praise he has to offer is sandwiched in the middle of the piece, the place where it has the least impact. The opening and closing sentences talk of 'watered-down' and 'left for dead'.

Crucial to the structure of reviews is the way in which you arrange your blocks of positive and negative comment. The worst solution, because it leaves your readers feeling dizzy, is to zigzag from one to the other throughout the review: 'This is great, but on the other hand, but then again, but then again . . . ' It is clearer to have substantial blocks of points in favour and points against.

For instance, if you are reviewing a novel, it is best to avoid slaloming your way around every single aspect of the book – plot, characters, style, form, message, and so on – allocating plus and minus points to each. Instead, you should first put aside the least significant or interesting aspects, then, with what you have left, create solid building blocks of praise and condemnation, regardless of the aspect being praised or condemned. Thus you might, in one block, praise a novel for its prose style, intelligence and humour and, in another, criticise its political insensitivity, for instance.

How you arrange these, however, can vary. Reviewing a book you enjoyed a lot, you might decide to open with praise, have a small block of negative comment in the middle, then finish with another substantial block of praise. Or you might decide to open with what you think is wrong with it (but expressing it in such a way that your readers can guess a 'but' is coming), then move into a substantial block of praise that continues to the end. Or, if what you dislike is trivial, you could position the negative comment as a fleeting parenthesis at the end: 'The novel may lack the full-throttle pace and finely tuned plotting of its predecessor, but the raucous humour is still firing on all cylinders.'

You will also need to decide where to place the basic factual information. Depending on the convention of your newspaper or magazine, some of this may be given, as a matter of course, at the top of the review. Reviews of single books, for instance, will usually begin with the title, the name of the author(s), the publisher and price. But this still may not be enough. Readers seeing: '*Déjà Dead* by Kathy Reich (Heinemann £10)' will not immediately know who Reich is, whether her book is non-fiction or fiction, or what its subject matter is. You need to tell them. The question is, when?

The answer is, pretty quickly. This need not necessarily mean in the opening sentence or paragraph (see 'Intros', below) but certainly before you proceed with any kind of detailed criticism.

Extra thought is needed if you are writing a round-up review: of the highlights from last night's television, the month's new movies, the best in recent science fiction or whatever. For this, you will need to consider how to make the elements work together, including the order in which they should be placed.

Where order is concerned, there are two straightforward solutions. You could either start with the programme, film or novel you liked most, allocating it the greatest share of words, and proceed downwards (in liking and word-length) from there. Or you could start with the most newsworthy, the one of which most of your readers will have heard, the one by the most famous artist, and, again, work downwards from there. But these are not the only options. To take just one example: you might choose to allocate the greatest share of words to the programme, film or novel you most hated. If that seems appropriate, do it.

The other question is how to link the disparate elements of the review. If an overall theme suggests itself, pick it up and run with it. If, however, the works have little in common, then rather than try to crush them into a framework in which they are uncomfortable you might prefer to use minor links to attach one review to the next. For instance, in a round-up review of movies in *Harpers & Queen*, Hugo Williams finds a link like this. First, he ends his review of one film:

> The film [*Midnight in the Garden of Good and Evil*] is a series of marvellous visual jokes, not least the po-faced black coming-out ball, hilariously deconstructed by the unexpected arrival of the Lady Chablis [a black drag queen], sheathed in blue sequins.

Then he moves to the next review:

> It is a month of triumph for black actors. Pam Grier, star of a string of successful blaxploitation thrillers in the Seventies, read for the part eventually played by Rosanna Arquette in *Pulp Fiction*, and was reportedly pinching herself when an offer arrived for the name part in the new Tarantino movie, *Jackie Brown*.

If there are neither obvious links nor any obvious common theme, it is usually best not to push it. Simply type a full stop after one review, breathe, then proceed to the next.

PAST OR PRESENT TENSE?

Before you start writing, there is one small grammatical question to consider. Should you use the past tense or the present? The rule is more or less simple. Events that will have come and gone by the time the review is published – one-off concerts, for instance, or television or radio programmes – are usually described in the past tense:

> As adroitly as a snake charmer coaxing a sleepy cobra from its basket, he *persuaded* 98-year-old Frances Partridge, the last of the Bloomsbury group, to talk about her marriage. [My italics]
> Sue Arnold reviewing a programme in Michael Berkeley's Radio 3 series *Private Passions* in the *Observer*

The past tense could also be appropriate to describe an event at which something took place that will probably not be repeated: a performance of a play in which an understudy took over to rapturous applause, for instance.

Otherwise, the convention is to use the present tense:

> *It's* 1970 and the streets are thick with chaos during a state of emergency declared by General Franco's right-wing regime. En route to hospital, a prostitute *gives* birth on a bus . . . [My italics]
> Martin Aston reviewing Pedro Almodóvar's movie *Live Flesh* in *Neon*

INTROS

As with features, there are no rules about how a review should open – except that, as with all journalism, the words should snatch the reader's attention and be relevant, directly or obliquely, to the main point you intend to make. There are, however, a number of tried and tested formulas.

The most straightforward is to step straight in with the basic factual information referred to in 'Structure' above. Thus John Dugdale, reviewing a batch of crime novels in the *Sunday Times*, opens one review like this:

> Set in the winter of 1586–7, Patricia Finney's *Unicorn's Blood* asks why the Virgin Queen eventually succumbed to her advisers' pressure to execute Mary, Queen of Scots, and hypothesises that spymaster Walsingham blackmailed her after acquiring a confessional youthful journal.

This approach could be deadly dull. A careless (or maybe distracted) sub once changed a reviewer's opening sentence from 'This is an historical novel about historical novels' to the rather less provocative and interesting 'This is an historical novel'. But starting with the basic information works when it is unusual or arresting: in John Dugdale's case, first because thrillers are not often set in the sixteenth century; second because of the widespread fascination with Mary, Queen of Scots. Describing Walsingham as a 'spymaster' also attracts attention. Calling him 'secretary of state', although no less truthful, would be less arresting.

In the same column, Dugdale reviews the Kathy Reich novel referred to in 'Structure' above. Here, although again he opens with the basic, factual information, he gives it a critical twist.

> Kathy Reich's *Déjà Dead* is so undisguisedly a DIY Patricia Cornwell novel that part of the considerable enjoyment of reading it lies in ticking off the formulaic features.

Crime-fiction fans will immediately know what a Patricia Cornwell novel is: will know that her regular heroine is a feisty forensic scientist who time and again solves gruesome murders before the mystified police can. Assuming that most of his readers will be fans, Dugdale has therefore taken the risk of using a form of shorthand in his opening sentence (although, later, he does go on to explain more fully what he means). But the main point to note is that he has judged the novel's subject – forensic scientist solves serial murder – too routine to open the review without the addition of that critical twist.

'They [critics] search for ages for the wrong word which, to give them credit, they eventually find.'
    Peter Ustinov

Another straightforward way to begin is with a summing-up of your judgement:

> This is a magical and magisterial production by Adrian Noble: one of the finest accounts I've seen of a magical and magisterial play . . .
> John Peter reviewing *The Tempest* in the *Sunday Times*

> One of the freshest-sounding singles this year has arrived . . .
> Matt Munday reviewing Doris Day's *To Ulrike M* in the *Big Issue*

> *Jackie Brown* is fun . . .
> Alexander Walker in the London *Evening Standard*

You may, however, prefer to create suspense: to keep your readers waiting for both the basic facts and your judgement. One way is to drop them immediately into the heart of the experience.

> Nine men packing shotguns storm the old house at the edge of town. They are there to rout out the women. Teach them a lesson. Kill them.
> Fiona Morrow reviewing Toni Morrison's *Paradise* in *Time Out*

> Inside the Roundhouse at Chalk Farm, shining like a huge paper lantern in the enclosing dark, is this truncated, spiral, vision thing, conspicuously clean, with walls in white nylon and a fresh soft-wood scent, strong enough to overcome, almost, the smell of old dirt.
> William Feaver reviewing an installation by The Kabakovs in the *Observer*

As long as the image you select is strong, readers will be prepared to wait for a context or an explanation.

Or you might decide to open with the visceral *feel* of the thing you are reviewing:

> A dense, thudding read that pumps its message home with the deliberation of a master sound system . . .
> J B Woolford reviewing Mark Hudson's *The Music in My Head* in *Pride*

Or – this opening is frequently used – you might decide on a teasing or provocative statement:

> The charms of crockery can be overlooked . . .
> Tibor Fischer reviewing Janet Gleeson's *The Arcanum* in the *Mail on Sunday*

> There are not enough sounds on the stage nowadays.
> Susannah Clapp reviewing Nancy Meckler's production of *I Am Yours* in the *Observer*

> Wife swapping will be the main topic of conversation at dinner parties this month.
> Charlie Higson reviewing Ang Lee's *The Ice Storm* in *Red*

Or you might start with a relevant anecdote, personal or otherwise:

> Nobody, it seems, bothers to read *Ulysses* nowadays. On a recent *Tea Junction* on Radio 4, the novelist Michael Dobbs remarked that he had yet to meet anyone who had finished it.
> John Carey reviewing *James Joyce and Censorship* in the *Sunday Times*

> I have come away from gigs exhilarated. I have come away from gigs disappointed. I've even come away from gigs held in a headlock by bouncers.
> Barbara Ellen reviewing a Cornershop concert in the *Observer*

Jokes, quotes, questions: a review may begin with any of these. Sooner rather than later, however, you must get round to telling the reader *what* it is you are reviewing.

HOW TO EXPRESS YOUR OPINION

You have written the opening paragraph. Either in it, or shortly after, you have explained what it is you are reviewing. Now for the bulk of the review.

Perhaps the most important point to consider as you continue writing is the need to justify your assertions with illustration, explanation or argument. Except when the word-length is really tight, it is not enough to declare baldly that such-and-such a movie is 'funny'. You need to quote lines or describe a scene illustrating the funniness. The reasons for this are several. First, an example is usually more vivid to read than a simple statement. Second, you may find that, when you search for a suitable example, you are forced to reconsider, modify or even change your assertion.

Third, you owe it to the reader and the work you are reviewing. However informed or intelligent your opinions, you must never believe they are absolute. So, by describing what you find funny, you allow room for readers to conclude that your sense of humour and theirs are different. Similarly, were you to decide that a book was 'a load of macho nonsense', you would need to provide enough evidence of this for your readers to calculate to what extent your idea of nonsense corresponds with theirs.

Should you, therefore, keep repeating 'In my opinion' or 'I felt'? No: a review is transparently an expression of the writer's opinion. You may need to declare an interest. You should, for instance, make it clear if the director of the play you are reviewing is your mother. Or, if reviewing a collection of gay erotic poetry, you might well conclude that your sexuality needed spelling out (even your sex, if your by-line left that ambiguous). But to keep insisting 'This is just my opinion' is redundant and faintly annoying.

'Writing about art is like dancing about architecture.'
    Anon

Next: avoid empty adjectives. 'Brilliant', 'beautiful', 'awful' and so on are the sounds of someone flailing in the dark. Consider *why* you think something is awful (or brilliant, or beautiful or whatever), then tell your readers.

You can even convey a judgement through description alone. Take, for instance, this sentence from a Nicola Barker restaurant review in the *Observer*: 'The meal begins with tubs of steaming hot, ripe-as-all-hell tomato and nippy mint soup with chunks of butter-drenched walnut bread.' There is no need for Barker to add that the soup tasted delicious. The description has made that clear.

'I can take any amount of criticism, so long as it is unqualified praise.'
Noël Coward

Praise is a delight to receive but not easy to give. Even experienced critics, reviewing something they have loved, are prone to lose themselves and their readers in a mist of vacuous superlatives. The solution is to be as clear, precise and specific as you can – taking the time to analyse exactly what it was that gave you pleasure.

That said, it is widely agreed that praise is harder to write than knocking copy. A good insult springs from the fingers with such a satisfying elegance. Consider how gratified Mary McCarthy must have felt as she typed this condemnation of fellow writer Lillian Hellman:

Every word she writes is a lie, including 'and' and 'the'.

Or what about this, from the nineteenth-century critic Eugene Field reviewing a production of *King Lear*:

He played the King as though under momentary apprehension that someone else was about to play the Ace.

BEWARE OF LIBEL

If you truthfully feel that adverse comment is in order, then by all means go ahead. But do take care that your insults are appropriate and relevant. Insulting a performer's physical appearance, for instance, is relevant only if it has direct bearing on the work. Moreover, as a critic, *you are not immune to the libel laws.*

You do have a defence to the charge, which you share with columnists and satirists. It is known as 'fair comment'. According to this you may, paradoxically, be as *unfair* as you want, so long as whatever you write is your 'honest opinion'. But this is where things get dangerous.

First, opinion is not the same as fact. You would be perfectly entitled, for instance, to write that the crowd scenes in a production of Shakespeare's *Julius Caesar* gave the impression that Rome contained only three plebeians. But were you to write that the crowds were composed of three actors, when in fact they were composed of five, you would have no defence to libel.

Second, if your opinion is way over the top, it might be concluded that it could not be 'honest'. Libel suits against reviewers are rare, but a successful one was brought against a columnist whose comments on the size of an actress's bum were judged not only factually wrong but far too excessive to be 'honest'.

Third, you must not be motivated by malice. Should your bastard of an ex-lover publish a collection of poetry, do not, whatever you do, review it. Were you to write that their sense of rhythm had obviously not improved, you would have no defence to libel.

The fourth test of 'honest opinion' is that you should be commenting on a matter of public interest. This should not usually worry you, since a published work or a public performance is obviously of public interest. But it does raise another, non-legal, question. Critics disagree about this, but to me it seems there is little point in slamming artists so obscure that, were it not for your reviewing their work, your readers would be blithely unaware of them. Would it not be better to leave them in the shadows?

NAME THE ARTIST

Condemning or praising, you should usually name the people singled out. This may seem obvious if the artist in question is a famous chef, the lead singer in a band, the star of a show, the author of a book. But it also applies to translators, arrangers, set designers, and so on. If you think the lighting made an important contribution to a ballet, name the designer.

'As a swashbuckling Cyrano, Mr Woodward's performance buckles more often than it swashes.'
    Kenneth Hurren

For actors, there are two conventions, depending on the structure of the sentence. If it is structured like Kenneth Hurren's quote above, with the actor given more importance than the role, then you simply name him as you would any other artist whose work you were mentioning. If, however, it is the role that has most importance in the sentence, then the actor's name is usually inserted in brackets: 'Ulysses Jackson (Peter Fonda) works as a beekeeper in the tupelo marshes of rural Florida . . . '

SPOILING THE SUSPENSE

At the end of Agatha Christie's theatrical whodunnit *The Mousetrap*, audiences are asked to keep the murderer's identity a secret so as not to spoil the suspense for those who have yet to see the play. Should critics generally refrain from revealing twists, surprises and dénouements?

There are two schools of thought about this. The first holds that of course they should, that anything else would wreck the enjoyment of potential audiences and readers. The second holds that, since a review is not an advertising trailer, it is entirely legitimate to reveal whatever the critic likes. This is something you will need to decide for yourself.

ENDINGS

The end of a review is usually a summing-up of the critic's opinion:

> But if you admire Nick Hornby's grasp of the easy comedy of life, recognise the universal truths he divines through a pop-cultural lens, and appreciate the deft interplay between mismatched everymen (the single-parent's kid, the thirtysomething loafer), you'll love this.
> Craig McLean reviewing Nick Hornby's *About A Boy* in *The Face*

> Something is badly amiss here, though, and it's the labour rather than the love that weighs on you at the end.
> Anthony Quinn reviewing the movie *Oscar and Lucinda* in the *Mail on Sunday*

> Like I said, refreshing. Just don't get too famous, lads.
> Lisa Mullen reviewing a Tortoise gig in *Time Out*

> This is not a novel to be tossed aside lightly. It should be thrown with great force.
> Dorothy Parker

No rules dictate this formulation. But skim as many reviews as you like and you will see that they might as well. In other words, you may end a review in whatever way you see fit but, if you find it *difficult* to end, then summing up your opinion is as good a solution as any. Besides, you will make life easier for lazy or hard-pressed readers, who know that skipping to the end of a review will usually tell them, if nothing else, whether to get their wallet out.

HOW TO GET IN

To become the regular film critic for a national paper or glossy magazine takes time, experience and contacts. The same is true should you wish to become a regular critic of any sort for a prestigious, well-paying media outlet. Such jobs are rarely available to young or inexperienced journalists. Moreover, reviewers are not, in general, among the best-paid journalists. They get to see a lot of movies, keep a lot of CDs and books but, even if they have the luck to be on a salary or long-term contract, they are unlikely to become millionaires.

There is more bad news. Because so many young writers are interested in the arts, the competition for reviewing work is intense. But there is good news too.

Youth can work to your advantage. Most publications prefer to have younger journalists reviewing pop music and clubs. Less obviously, a literary editor may specifically want a young reviewer for a book aimed at the youth market or written by a young author.

Specialist knowledge or special experience can also be a useful spring-board. If, for instance, you know all there is to know about drum'n'bass, then you are in a stronger position than someone with casual, generalised musical knowledge. Similarly, if you have experience of accounting, snow-boarding, being the child of alcoholic parents or whatever, you have a good case to put to a literary editor with a book on one of those subjects awaiting review. Or, if you live out of London and know your way round the local music, theatre, dance, club or art scene, you could be useful to arts editors fed up with trying to persuade staff journalists to travel.

The crucial thing is to keep abreast of what is happening in your chosen field; by and large editors know about the immediate and the mainstream. Ask publishers to send you their catalogues. Keep in touch with your local theatres, music venues, clubs. Read specialist publications. Surf the Internet. Hang out with people who work in the arts. And, if you get a job as a sub, editorial assistant or reporter, but would like to be writing reviews as well or instead, make frequent visits to the arts desk to enquire about what is coming up.

Finally, although you should study the style and approach of whatever publication you would like to review for, you should never, ever, try to reproduce its critics' opinions. Your views, your take on things, are what matter – both to commissioning editors and to yourself. They are why people will want to employ you. They are what give you your individual voice. They are why you want to be a critic.

'Has anyone ever seen a dramatic critic in the daytime? Of course not. They come out after dark, up to no good.'
   P G Wodehouse

The ways in to reviewing may be obscure and hard to locate but, if you look hard enough, they are there.

WHY BOTHER?

The question is: why bother?

'Pay no attention to what the critics say. No statue has ever been put up to a critic.'
   Jean Sibelius

If you want to be a hero, do not become a critic. Creative artists hate critics. Readers delight in arguing with them. History loves looking back at them and sneering at what they got wrong. The only reason to write reviews is that you enjoy the art or entertainment form about which you write, enjoy being forced to consider why such a thing works and such a thing does not, enjoy trying to convey your experience in words.

If, when you were a child, someone had told you that you could earn money by cuddling up with a succession of books; sitting transfixed in the cinema; going to the theatre, the ballet, the opera, rock concerts; eating out in restaurants; watching television; watching videos; listening to CDs: what would have been your reaction? If you would have shrugged, forget reviewing. If you would have laughed with amazement, go for it.

TWO REVIEWS

Adam Mars-Jones reviewing Sebastian Barry's novel *The Whereabouts of Eneas McNulty* in the *Observer*:

> Sebastian Barry's new novel is so full of magnetising beauty that it all but harasses a reader into submission. You can try to protest, to

say, 'I'm a reader and you're a book, can we not keep this on a professional basis?' but the book won't have it so. *The Whereabouts of Eneas McNulty* is Barry's first novel for 10 years, and during that decade he has made a major mark with his plays, but in these pages he seems most like a poet. Many sentences seem actively to yearn for an uneven right-hand margin to point up their rhythms and designs: 'The cold desert in his mind's eye floods with the thousand small white flowers that are the afterlife of rainfall.'

Eneas McNulty is born in Sligo at the turn of the century, first child of a Catholic jobbing tailor, who met his seamstress wife-to-be in the asylum where he worked running up clothing for the inmates. Eneas is dispossessed for the first time when more children come along, but is consoled by friendship with an older boy, Jonno Lynch.

At 16, for no reason except the need to find a place for himself, and a vague desire to rescue poor, suffering France, Eneas joins the British Merchant navy. His taking of the King's shilling is not a political decision: in a striking phrase applied to the proprietor of the Great Western Hotel in Athlone, he − and the book which contains him − might be described as being 'above politics and beneath neutrality'.

After the war Eneas compounds his error of affiliation by joining the Royal Irish Constabulary and brands himself, in the changing political climate, definitively traitor. He isn't so stupid as not to know 'why there are places in the peelers when there are places nowhere else' but he can hardly predict the slow fuse of hatred that will follow him down the decades. Sentence of death is confirmed by Jonno, by the dear friend estranged. Eneas becomes a sort of sorrowful human comet, travelling in a highly elliptical orbit far from Sligo, in search of a place and an occupation − fishing, farming, digging − but returning at long intervals to whizz, grieving, past his family. He must part from the woman he loves, and never finds a substitute for her. Eneas may be named after a hero whose wanderings were ordained and finally rewarded, but he himself finds no home to replace the one he lost.

If Barry's prose is poetry carried on by other means, he is an unfashionable sort of poet, drawing images almost exclusively from the natural world, seen as a teeming library of images, mainly redemptive: 'The salmon is as clean as a pig in its nature, though unlike the pig it will not lie down in the dirt that men force on it.'

Eneas isn't an articulate man as the world sees it, but like all the characters in the book he has his own eloquence. Sweetly reproached by his pappy for his poor performance as a corres-pondent, he replies wryly: 'The writing hand is a rusty hand, that's true.' There are times when Barry misses blarney by only a leprechaun's whisker – when it occurs to Eneas that his pappy is 'a bit of a fool, a bit of a colossal fool' – but there's no doubt that the book is a stylistic triumph. And yet the truth is that the infinite distinction of the writing becomes limitation, almost, since the primal delight adheres to the separate sentences rather than the story they carry. The urge to read on is not really a desire to know what happens to the hero next, but to see what new marvels of phrasing Barry will breed from his stock of pet words.

Eneas's character is distinctly idealised, suffering and bewildered but exempted from serious internal tensions. He meets hatred with weariness but without embitterment. He is less an exile than an involuntary citizen of the world. He suffers mightily, but the prose in which his days and doings are suspended is balm for the reader if not for him. Readers of the book, gratified, selfish, may wish its hero well in a dim sort of way, but would happily see Eneas driven to the top of the barest crag, if that would guarantee his being struck a few thousand more times by the loving lightning of his maker's language.
Observer, 15 March 1998

The structure of this is classic. It opens by jumping forward with the visceral *feel* of the book (while deftly telling, or reminding, readers who the author is), then steps back to provide an outline of the plot and to hint at the themes. This is followed by the bulk of the assessment, helpfully illustrated with quotations. It makes both negative and positive points, but ends on the one that Mars-Jones thinks most important (with which he also opened the review): that the novel's language is beautiful.

His own language is precise and vivid, too. Look, for instance, at that final sentence. And notice how, as an *Observer* writer, he compliments his readers by assuming they have heard of the wandering Trojan hero Aeneas and will recognise the quotation about the relationship of war to diplomacy that he echoes in 'If Barry's prose is poetry carried on by other means . . . '. Most important, though, is that the review provides such a potent *sense* of the novel that readers will know very well, by the end, whether or not they want to read it.

Sylvia Patterson on Tori Amos's album *From the Choirgirl Hotel* in *Frank*:

She is 34 and still believes in fairies. She was raped at gunpoint and still believes in love. She is Tori Amos, 'bonkers banshee piano woman', purveyor of lyrical paeans to the joys of giving God a blow job, and a multi-million-selling 'cult' artiste with the sort of fame which spawns devoted 'fans' who hide in bushes with guns. Thus, as with all extremists, many people (especially boys) cannot be doing with Tori Amos, for she is a wailing siren who sings about blood clots running down your inner thighs – but, of course, these males are crybaby saps who are terrified of women's (sometimes literal) innards.

This time, however, after the chilling 1996 *Boys for Pele* (which signalled 'a change in my relationship with men for good'), she comes to us a glittery-eyed newly wed. But don't be looking for 'love-is-a-many-splendoured-thing' here. She is also a soul-shattered mother-to-be who miscarried her baby in 1997. *From the Choirgirl Hotel* is the story of how she coped and how she didn't and how, in the end, she found a brand-new passion for Life. And how, while she was at it, she found herself a band of musically gifted snooksters with whom she expanded her spiky piano dramatics into whole new dimensions of soundscape terror and epic gorgeousness. Which, at least once (on the baying *Cruel*), has turned her into Patti Smith guesting on a particularly 'dark' Tricky song.

This is Amos's shock-free album, featuring no artwork treats like piglets being suckled on her breast (as she did inside *Boys for Pele*); on this sleeve she floats in blackness, with her hands engaged in some flaky-fingered Ted Rogers '321' impersonation (but more likely the magic signalling of Inca binary charms, or some such). So, she's free, and, in freedom, brings us her version of the ubiquitous late-90s epic with a different kind of lyric: 'She's addicted to nicotine patches' goes the hairy *Spark*; 'She's afraid of a light in the dark . . . but she couldn't keep baby alive.' And in *Playboy Mommy* she sings to the spirit of what she was sure was going to be her daughter: 'Don't judge me so harsh little girl . . . you gotta playboy mommy.'

It's sorrow set, however, to some of the most beautiful sounds Amos has ever conjured from her kaleidoscopic mind: the rousing *Raspberry Swirl*, the mournful loveliness of *Liquid Diamonds*, the frankly hysterical *She's Your Cocaine* and the goose-bump caper of *Northern Lad* which breaks your heart in 47 places and then makes you want to leap naked off the top of an Icelandic volcano brimful of finest Viking vodka.

Her voice, too, has found a new fandango to dance. The vocal gymnastics of *Hotel* are berserk to behold, before she coos, 'I'm still alive . . . I'm still alive . . . I'm still alive.' Tori Amos is, in actual fact, one of those rare people who is Truly Alive; positively exploding, in fact, with life. It is this which makes her 'mad', which is to say she has a personality, big ideas, a bigger heart, and a wise head and something to say about rock'n'roll and pain and sacrifice and joy. *From the Choirgirl Hotel* is the first Tori Amos album you can dance to (on the right kind of drugs). You could even have sex to it and not feel squiffy afterwards. It is more P J Harvey and

Portishead than Kate Bush, and the furthest away from the 'mad-
woman-with-a-piano' stereotype she has ever been; it's over the
lone-piano wall into the multi-layered atmospheric pool of Joni
Mitchell and the technology of Massive Attack. And, like all the
best ideas, you wonder why she didn't think of it before.
Frank, June 1998

Although this is very different in voice from Adam Mars-Jones's review
above, it shares with it the power to make readers experience what the
reviewer experienced, to feel the reviewer's enthusiasm and to know, by
the end, whether or not the work of art is their kind of thing. This review
opens by talking, at length, about the artist: not only because the facts
of her life are attention-grabbing but because the album is, in effect, a
chapter of her autobiography. The assessment component which follows
is apparently nothing but positive, but the odd tongue-in-cheek phrase –
'more likely the magic signalling of Inca binary charms, or some such'
– concedes that the album might sometimes veer towards pretentious-
ness.

Patterson's language is sometimes more inventive than correct
– 'musicianly gifted snooksters' – but never incomprehensible. And
although she does, at one point, describe Amos's 'sounds' as 'beautiful',
she immediately specifies what she means: 'the goose-bump caper of
Northern Lights which breaks your heart in 47 places . . .'. (The side-
swipes at 'boys' and 'crybaby' men in the opening paragraph are there at
least in part because *Frank* is a magazine aimed at women.)

5
Style

MURDER YOUR DARLINGS

The traditional view on English style is simply put. Be clear; avoid ornament; let the message reveal itself. From Samuel Johnson and Jonathan Swift in the eighteenth century to George Orwell in the twentieth, the literary critics and experts on writing have agreed. Style is not something to be strained for or added on: it is there in the writer – or the subject – waiting to be expressed. What is needed is plainness, decorum, economy, precision – above all, clarity. What is not needed is rhetoric or embellishment.

Quoting a college tutor Dr Johnson pronounced: 'Read over your compositions, and where ever you meet with a passage which you think is particularly fine, strike it out.' And echoing Dr Johnson, Sir Arthur Quiller-Couch told Cambridge undergraduates in 1913: 'Whenever you feel an impulse to perpetrate a piece of exceptionally fine writing, obey it – whole-heartedly – and delete it before sending your manuscript to press. *Murder your darlings.*'

As his Oxford opposite number, J Middleton Murry, noted a few years later, 'These *obiter dicta* of the masters . . . all point the same way; they all lay stress solely on the immediate nature of style; they all reduce the element of art or artifice to nothingness.'

'Proper words in proper places make the true definition of a style.'
  Jonathan Swift

A famous campaigner for simple English, Sir Ernest Gowers, wrote an influential book intended to help civil servants in their use of written English – he called it *Plain Words*. It is full of passages like

The most prevalent disease in present-day writing is a tendency to say what one has to say in as complicated a way as possible. Instead of being simple, terse and direct, it is stilted, long-winded and circumlocutory; instead of choosing the simple word it prefers the unusual; instead of the plain phrase, the cliché.

In the United States the traditional message has been exactly the same. William Strunk, whose book *The Elements of Style* was later revised by E B White, wrote in 1918:

Young writers often suppose that style is a garnish for the meat of prose, a sauce by which a dull dish is made palatable. Style has no such separate entity; it is non-detachable, unfilterable. . . . The approach to style is by way of plainness, simplicity, orderliness, sincerity.

This emphasis on plainness and simplicity has been repeated by those who lay down the law about journalistic style. *The Economist Pocket Style Book*, first published in the 1980s, quotes George Orwell's 'six elementary rules' from a famous essay, 'Politics and the English Language', written in 1946:

1   Never use a metaphor, simile or other figure of speech which you are used to seeing in print.
2   Never use a long word where a short word will do.
3   If it is possible to cut out a word, always cut it out.
4   Never use the passive where you can use the active.
5   Never use a foreign phrase, a scientific word or a jargon word if you can think of an everyday English equivalent.
6   Break any of these rules sooner than say anything outright barbarous.

THE FOG INDEX

The Americans, who take journalism education and training more seriously than the British, have developed a systematic way of measuring the readability of newspapers and magazines. The journalism trainer Robert Gunning gave his name in 1944 to the Gunning Fog Index, which sets out to show how clear or obscure ('foggy') writing is.

The index is based on counting the long words and working out the length of an average sentence in a sample passage. A formula translates this into the approximate number of years of education needed to understand it. The higher the fog index, the harder the passage is to understand.

'Have something to say, and say it as clearly as you can. That is the only secret of style.'
Matthew Arnold

Thus a popular American TV magazine scores 6, equivalent to sixth grade or six years of education, while the *Ladies' Home Journal* scores 8, the *National Geographic* 10, and *Time* magazine 12 – equivalent to high school senior or 12 years of education.

Some British trainers apply the index to our media: a typical airport novel would score 6, a downmarket tabloid (the *Mirror*) 8–10, a middle-market tabloid (the *Express*) 10–12, a broadsheet (the *Telegraph*) 12–14, a specialist periodical (*Pulse*) 14–16 – and the small print in an insurance company document 20.

Whether or not you adopt the index, the idea that underlies it is essential: to write successfully for a publication you must write so that its readers understand you.

WRITE THE WAY YOU TALK

In the orthodox Anglo-American tradition there is a second command-ment: that good writing should mirror speech rather than aspire to be something else, something artificial, contrived, self-consciously literary. As William Hazlitt put it in the early nineteenth century,

> To write a genuine familiar or true English style is to write as any-one would speak in common conversation, who had a thorough command and choice of words, or who could discourse with ease, force and perspicuity, setting aside all pedantic and oratorical flourishes.

Later, Cyril Connolly attacked what he called the mandarin style

> beloved by literary pundits, by those who would make the written word as unlike as possible to the spoken one. It is the style of those writers whose tendency is to make their language convey more than they mean or more than they feel, it is the style of most artists and all humbugs.

'As to the Adjective: when in doubt, strike it out.'
Mark Twain

Both Hazlitt and Connolly were journalists – and their message has been enthusiastically endorsed by later experts on journalistic style. Harold

Evans in his classic *Newsman's English* quotes Connolly with approval and recommends 'a clear, muscular and colloquial style'; Nicholas Bagnall in *Newspaper Language* quotes Hazlitt and calls his 'the best definition I know of the true language of journalism'.

In one of his 10 principles of clear statement Robert Gunning takes the argument a stage further and urges 'Write the way you talk', while John Whale in his book *Put It in Writing* repeats the point in more formal British English – 'Write as you speak'.

For all sorts of reasons – including the powerful influence on print of TV and radio – this link between the spoken word and journalistic writing is now stronger than ever.

METAPHORS ARE MORE FUN

Both these ideas – write plainly and clearly; write as you speak – are obviously relevant to anyone learning journalism. The first is essential in basic news writing and instructional copy (telling readers how to mend a fuse, make an omelette, fill in a tax form). But that is not the end of the matter.

Unfortunately – in journalism as in writing generally – the rule is often assumed to apply across the board, whereas it does not. Good style cannot be reduced to the slogan 'Write plainly and clearly'.

As the American writer Richard Lanham points out in a little-known but forceful attack on the classics, *Style: An Anti-Textbook*: 'People seldom write simply to be clear. They have designs on their fellow men. Pure prose is as rare as pure virtue, and for the same reasons.'

Lanham ridicules The Books for preaching that the best style is the never-noticed, for recommending that prose style should, like the state under Marxism, wither away, leaving the plain facts shining unto themselves. 'People, even literary people, seldom content themselves with being clear. They invent jargons, argot . . . and even when they succeed in being clear it is often only to seem clever.'

It is not easy to find examples of great writers who wrote 'plainly and clearly'. Certainly not the poets Chaucer, Shakespeare, Keats, Eliot; and not the novelists from Fielding to Martin Amis by way of Dickens and Lawrence. Even the literary preachers didn't always practise plainness. Dr Johnson was famously florid rather than plain; Swift, the scourge of looseness and incorrectness, often got carried away.

'There are no dull subjects. There are only dull writers.'
H L Menken

On the other hand, George Orwell, journalist, novelist, literary critic, is perhaps the best exponent of the plain style in English literature. His work is content-driven and in many ways he provides an excellent model of control, simplicity and precision.

Then of course there is Ernest Hemingway, master story-teller, Nobel prizewinner, another novelist who started as a journalist – his style is famous for its apparent simplicity. Here's a paragraph from his last great book, *The Old Man and the Sea*:

> The old man had seen many great fish. He had seen many that weighed more than a thousand pounds and he had caught two of that size in his life, but never alone. Now alone, and out of sight of land, he was fast to the biggest fish that he had ever seen and bigger than he had ever heard of, and his left hand was still as tight as the gripped claws of an eagle.

Note that word 'apparent' applied to 'simplicity': here is the use of deliberate repetition (for example, 'had seen many' repeated early on), the characteristic use of 'and' (three times in the last sentence), the gradual increase in sentence length, all contributing to a rich and powerful rhythm. The paragraph ends with the simile of the eagle's claws – which stands out from the 'plainness' of the rest.

Hemingway's prose then is not as simple as it looks. Other great writers of the twentieth century have been dense (Faulkner), ornate (Nabakov) – or just plain difficult (Joyce).

As in literature so in personal life, politics, business, advertising – how can anybody argue that all speakers and writers aspire to clarity first and foremost? Of course, they have to be *capable* of clarity and know when to use it. But they don't use it all the time, not if they are arguing a case, wooing a woman or a man, playing a scene for laughs, showing off, selling a secondhand car . . .

Then there is the delight that so many speakers and writers take in playing with words. As Lanham puts it:

> People seldom content themselves with plain utterance even in daily life. It gets boring. . . . They prefer the metaphorical, the indirect expression to the straightforward, literal one. They are not trying to be literary. Metaphors are just more fun.

CLARITY, CLARITY, CLARITY*

But there is a strong – indeed overwhelming – argument that, whatever politicians, lovers and secondhand car dealers may do, journalists must be clear above all; that journalism has no point otherwise; that an essential part of its function is to interrogate the politicians and conmen, to represent and communicate with the ordinary person confronted by authority, salesmanship, jargon, pretention . . . Journalism must be clear.

Individual words and phrases must be clear so that your reader can understand them. For example, you must be careful with technical terms – a word suitable for a specialist periodical might be too abstruse for a daily paper. And, just as important, anything you write must be clear in structure: you must say things in the right order – without aimlessly repeating yourself or digressing too far from your main point.

'If a rule of writing has been constantly broken by good writers, it is no rule.'
        John Whale

Does this mean that the traditionalists are right after all? For journalism (as opposed to other kinds of writing) do we have to go back to the slogan 'Write plainly and clearly'?

Certainly, if journalism could be reduced to plainness and clarity, life would be much simpler and well-edited listings pages could stand as the perfect model of good style. But obviously this won't do. So we have to think again.

Plainness and clarity are associated for two reasons. First, to repeat the point, there are certain kinds of journalistic writing (basic news, instructional copy) where they belong together. Second, the easiest, safest way to achieve clarity is by plainness: avoid frills and you can be confident you will get your meaning across without having to strain too hard.

This is why trainee journalists are instructed to write plainly: to learn to walk before they start running. And this is why style manuals that concentrate on the basics tend to elaborate Orwell's 'six elementary rules' into the Ten Commandments of Plain Writing – each one to do with

---

* This heading is in fact a quotation from *The Elements of Style*: it is clear – but the rhetoric of repetition makes it far from plain.

keeping it simple and cutting out clutter. (*English for Journalists*, which includes a chapter on style, takes this general approach.)

The point is not that these instructions are wrong but that they are incomplete: plainness is not all. For if we distinguish between plainness and clarity, we can see that journalism – though it must have clarity – should not necessarily be plain. It should be plain where plainness is a virtue – as in basic news and instructional copy – and it should be coloured where colour is called for.

A PERSONAL STYLE

Feature writers, for example, often develop a strongly personal style – opinionated, anecdotal, gossipy. Columnists and gossip writers cannot do without one. People like Julie Burchill and Bernard Levin are celebrated – and paid – as much for their style as for their content. They are read because people enjoy their word play and tricks of style.

Here is Burchill, who started her journalistic career as a punk music writer on *NME* and has written columns for, among others, the *Mail on Sunday*, the *Sunday Times* and the *Guardian*:

> Ever since the mid-Eighties, desperate hippies with haircuts have tried to rewrite and reclaim punk as the last gasp of right-on rebellion. But it wasn't. It was rebellious – but only in the way that Mrs Thatcher was. Punk was about a break with consensus. And we media brats, like our susser soulmates who would come up a few years later in the city – the Big Bang boys, which in itself sounded like a Malcolm McLaren concept group – were McLaren's and Thatcher's children. We were non-U upstarts with names like Steve and Paul and Julie and Debbie. And what we all shared was Attitude: short-haired, hyper-impatient, get-filthy-rich-quick, liberal-baiting and hippie-hating.

This extract from Burchill's autobiography *I Knew I Was Right*, serialised in the *Guardian*, states her position, of course – but it is fun to read whatever you think of it. Essentially, she performs – like the punk musicians she started off writing about.

'Style is more difficult than substance.'
    Roy Hattersley

Reviewers, on the other hand, are essentially people with opinions – the stronger the better. But a distinctive style is a great advantage to a reviewer because it can make their view of the work easy to grasp and remember – as well as making the review entertaining to read. If you read this kind of reviewer regularly, you get used to their attitudes and can more easily work out what you would think in their place.

Incidentally, there's no escaping the point that knocking review copy – like bad news – sells more papers than puffs do. Writers like Victor Lewis-Smith in the London *Evening Standard* and A A Gill in the *Sunday Times* have often been compulsive reading in their brutal destruction of mediocre television. Programme producers may not like it – but most readers do.

'[Style] consists simply of choosing a handful of words from the half a million or so samples available, and arranging them in the best order.'
Keith Waterhouse

Even news stories are sometimes written to tease, intrigue and entertain as well as to inform. And while instructional copy must remain plain and simple, the sections introducing it can be anything but.

Take cookery journalism, for example: recipes must be plain, step-by-step, no frills; but the writing that introduces the recipes is often evocative, atmospheric, allusive. Before readers get down to business in the kitchen, they want to be seduced by the scent of rosemary, the softness of raspberry, the crispness of celery, while all the time the Mediterranean murmurs in the background.

THE NEW JOURNALISM

And the new journalism, meaning the adoption by mainly American journalists of various experimental techniques from the mid-1960s onwards, is the opposite of plain. For example, Tom Wolfe, pioneer and joint editor of the definitive anthology *The New Journalism*, explains his lavish use of dots, dashes, exclamation marks, italics and so on as essentially FUN:

> I found a great many pieces of punctuation and typography lying around dormant when I came along – and I must say I had a good time using them. I figured it was time someone violated what Orwell called 'the Geneva conventions of the mind' . . . a protocol that had kept journalism and non-fiction generally (and novels) in such a tedious bind for so long.

Wolfe says that he and other New Journalists – Gay Talese, Truman Capote, Terry Southern, Hunter S Thompson, Joan Didion – gradually learnt the techniques of social realism developed by novelists such as Fielding, Balzac and Dickens. They adopted such devices as realistic dialogue and scene-by-scene construction (telling the story by moving from scene to scene rather than by historical narrative).

'With some writers, style not only reveals the spirit of the man, it reveals his identity, as surely as would his fingerprints.'
William Strunk

Effectively they were claiming for journalism territory previously occupied by the novel – and repudiating the claim that journalism was somehow inferior to the novel. They were also helping to dispose of the idea that good writing is necessarily plain and simple.

Here's a snippet from a celebrated piece on the Kentucky Derby by gonzo journalist Hunter S Thompson featuring the British cartoonist Ralph Steadman:

> I took the expressway out to the track, driving very fast and jumping the monster car back and forth between lanes, driving with a beer in one hand and my mind so muddled that I almost crushed a Volkswagen full of nuns when I swerved to catch the right exit. There was a slim chance, I thought, that I might be able to catch the ugly Britisher before he checked in.
>
> But Steadman was already in the press box when I got there, a bearded young Englishman wearing a tweed coat and HAF sunglasses. There was nothing particularly odd about him. No facial veins or clumps of bristly warts. I told him about the motel woman's description and he seemed puzzled. 'Don't let it bother you,' I said. 'Just keep in mind for the next few days that we're in Louisville, Kentucky. Not London. Not even New York. This is a weird place. You're lucky that mental defective at the motel didn't jerk a pistol out of the cash register and blow a big hole in you.' I laughed, but he looked worried.
> Scanlan's Monthly

'Gonzo', according to the dictionary, means 'bizarre, crazy, absurd'; is used about 'journalism of a subjective eccentric nature' – and, you might add, is certainly not politically correct. But, like the new journalism in general, this piece has life, colour and immediacy. Notice how specific it is: 'a Volkswagen full of nuns' rather than 'a carload of nuns'; 'a tweed coat and HAF sunglasses' rather than 'an overcoat and sunglasses'. Above all, it has the pace and rhythm of the spoken word. Clearly, the new journalism emphasises the continuity between speech and writing referred to above.

Earlier, the American journalist Studs Terkel developed a way of writing that took this link as far as it could be taken. His oral histories, such as *Working* and '*The Good War*' are essentially edited first-person accounts. But as he once admitted, the art is in finding the natural storytellers to interview: 'You don't just bump into anyone.'

BLAME THE TAPE-RECORDER

In less talented hands writing that reproduces speech authentically can be repetitive, obscure, unstructured – in a word, unreadable. For the worst examples blame the tape-recorder and, in particular, the interviewing style known as Q&A. In what can be a travesty of journalism as an active, inquiring, interpretive process the interviewer's role seems to consist of turning the tape on and off, asking the odd question, then typing up the transcript with a minimum of editing – and in the laziest cases getting somebody else to do even that.

Here's an extract from a Q&A with the French footballer Jean-Pierre Papin. As you read it you can hear the original French in which the interview was conducted:

TN: Are you thinking of coaching in the future?
JPP: I'm thinking of it. It needs a lot of experience.
TN: OK, but like many other high level sportsmen you have got the best experience on the pitch.
JPP: Managing a team is a different matter. I'm not ready yet.
TN: You are a 'fighter' on the ground. Is this the sort of quality you would expect from your players?
JPP: That's obviously what I would want from them.
TN: Why not in Bordeaux?
JPP: Why not indeed?

And so on – ad nauseam.

WRITE *BETTER* THAN YOU TALK

So reproducing speech as such can't be the answer to the style question. Indeed both Robert Gunning and John Whale ('Write the way you talk'/'Write as you speak') hedge more than a little when they go into detail.

The Gunning message (as outlined by his partner Douglas Mueller) turns into: 'Actually, we recommend that writers try to write *better* than they talk; to eliminate pauses, repetitions of words, and too many connectives. But the goal is to achieve a conversational tone.'

And Whale expands his slogan as follows:

> By this I mean that you should try to write as you would speak if you were talking at the top of your form, unhesitantly, in the idiom that best suited your theme and the occasion, and trusting your own ear.

To which you might object: but what if I have no top form to speak of, if I can't talk coherently and unhesitantly at the same time, if my ear is wooden and I don't feel able to trust it? Does it follow that I can't become a good writer?

Pushed to the limit, the Gunning-Whale argument fails. For there are certainly people who talk badly – hesitantly, repetitively, clumsily – but manage to write well. Some successful professional writers clearly do not write as they speak.

There is another, more general problem. Most people's speech has a looser grammar than their writing: sentences change direction without warning or are left unfinished; verbs don't agree with subjects; and so on. For most people, to follow the instruction 'write as you speak' would involve either reproducing the loose grammar of speech or having to go through the copy afterwards to tighten up the grammar.

'Write as you speak' turns out to be an overstatement of the obvious point that good written journalism has much in common with coherent speech. To put it another way, you don't really 'write as you speak', though to write well you may spend a lot of time and energy making it look as if you do.

WRITE WITH YOUR EARS

The simplest test of writing is certainly to read it out loud. You'll know immediately if sentences are too long: you won't have the puff to finish. You should be able to hear repetitions and clumsy constructions, too.

That is negative – a matter of avoiding mistakes. More positively, you should write with what is called cadence or rhythm. For example, write sentences that build to a powerful conclusion as this one from Dickens does:

It was my mother, cold and dead.

Here's a more elaborate example, also from Dickens:

> Annual income twenty pounds, annual expenditure nineteen nineteen six, result happiness. Annual income twenty pounds, annual expenditure twenty pounds ought and six, result misery.

A resignation note read simply:

> Hours too long, wages too low, life too short.

With his characteristic laconic style Julius Caesar reported to Rome:

> I came, I saw, I conquered.

And Dr Johnson produced this hard drinker's motto:

> Claret is the liquor for boys; port for men; but he who aspires to be a hero must drink brandy.

Writing in triplets like this works – the third element provides a punch-line. Similarly, where there are two related points to make, try to make your sentence balance, as in this example from Hazlitt (in the *Times*):

> The love of liberty is the love of others; the love of power is the love of ourselves.

This is antithesis: contrasting two opposite points. It often uses the rhetorical device of repetition: here the word 'love' does not become 'affection' or 'passion' in the second clause; if it did, the sentence would lose its power.

The point about repetition is that it should be intentional, serving a similar function to rhyme in verse. On occasion it can run right through a section. Here's an extract from a feature published at the height of the President Clinton–Monica Lewinsky scandal in 1998:

> Let's review what we've learned so far. The president a liar? *Knew that.*
>
> The president a philanderer? *Knew that.*
>
> The president reckless in the satisfaction of his appetites? *Knew that.*

> The president would say anything and hurt anybody to get out of a mess? *Knew that.*
>
> Married men cheat? *Knew that.*
>
> Hillary isn't throwing Bill's stuff on the White House lawn because she is as committed to their repugnant arrangement as he is? *Knew that.*
>
> The president has the nerve to pick out a dress for a woman. *Didn't know that . . .*
> New York Times

'Knew that' runs like a chorus through the section – until we get to the punchline. Also note that 'the president' is repeated (except where Hillary comes into the story and 'Bill' is used).

There is a danger in writing with your ears: what might be called the Hiawatha effect – getting stuck in one soporific rhythm, as in:

> By the shore of Gitche Gumee
> By the shining Big-Sea-Water
> Stood the wigwam of Nokomis
> Daughter of the Moon, Nokomis . . .

Except to make a particular point (or to parody Longfellow) do not write like this: vary your rhythms.

WORDS AND PHRASES

Words and phrases are the building blocks – and the flourishes – of writing. One single powerful word can transform a paragraph:

> Say what you like about the new ITV system that has arisen from the morass of the 1990 Broadcasting Act but you can't say it doesn't cater for minorities. GMTV, for example, caters for the brain-dead, a small but important proportion of the electorate whose needs have hitherto been addressed only by Rupert Murdoch.
> Observer

'Brain-dead' follows an innocuous-sounding sentence – which suddenly takes on a sharper meaning.

Next, here's a gossip writer in a London glossy commenting on objections by residents to a proposed memorial garden to Diana, Princess of Wales:

> It would be easy to deride the objectors for being cold-hearted but having seen the crowds, flowers and all those public tears, one can sympathise with Kensington residents who do not wish to walk out of their front door only to trip over some grieving wretch holding a bouquet.
> *London Portrait*

A fine example of 'writing for the reader': from the pompous misuse of 'deride' (the rest of us would say something like 'criticise' or 'condemn') to the strangulated 'one' (for 'you') this has the Kensington dialect to a tee. 'Grieving wretch' is superb.

'Look after the words and style will look after itself.'
Harold Evans

A fixation with words whether read or heard can be put to good use. Here's a bit from an interview with Gerry Adams, who admits to being nervous before speaking in public and being interviewed:

> 'Yes. All interviews.' Gerry Adams fixes a steady gaze, and says, slowly and deliberately, 'I urinate a *lot*.'

> There is something very particular about the word 'urinate'. It is a term people seldom use unless they're talking to a doctor. The kind of person who chooses to tell you that they urinate when nervous is normally the type to use words like 'tinkle' or 'waterworks'. But when Adams tells me that, he does so in the pared-down bald way characteristic of people who have endured extreme physical indignity; prisoners have it, and soldiers coming back from war.
> Decca Aitkenhead, *Guardian*

Or how about this?

> A recent trip to America has provided me with some splendid contemporary oxymorons to add to my already huge collection. I spotted 'airline food' before I'd even landed, and an airport menu furnished two more – 'jumbo shrimp' and 'this page intentionally left blank'. . . . My favourite was observed in Los Angeles: 'police protection'.
> Victor Lewis-Smith, London *Evening Standard*

Original vivid phrases are worth their weight: they stop you having to rely on the cliché. Here's one from a report on the British bodybuilding championships: the heavyweights are described as plodding on with gigantic thighs so big they impede movement . . .

> . . . and buns so tight you could bounce brussels sprouts off
> them.
> *Observer*

A vividly evoked picture: those huge bronzed, greased, muscly bottoms, elastically tight, and tiny green sprouts bouncing off them like squash balls – an attractively playful reaction to competitors who take themselves very seriously.

Successful phrases are often quirky, colourful, unexpected: they rely on contrast and conflict, the shock of the mismatched. For example, take a phrase and then – as though you'd landed on a snake during Snakes and Ladders – slide off somewhere surprising:

> The British do not fear change. Only this morning a young man
> asked me for some.
> Craig Brown parodying Tony Blair, *Daily Telegraph*

> The only thing men get at present-giving time is bitterly dis-
> appointed.
> *Ms London*

Or take a well-known phrase and turn it on its head:

> He was an opera fanatic, and the sort of man who gives that
> species a good name.
> Geoffrey Wheatcroft, *Opera*

> Only the young die good.
> Anon

Look for the unexpected, the vivid:

> 'She has Van Gogh's ear for music.'
> Alex McGregor quoting Billy Wilder, *Probe*

> 'Whoever writes his stuff deserves a place in Poets' Corner – as
> soon as possible.'
> Russell Davies, *Daily Telegraph*

Of a Serb militiaman manning a checkpoint in Bosnia:

> If I die and go to hell, I expect him to be there at the gates.
> Martin Bell, *Observer*

Of a character in a TV play:

A viper in peach silk and apricot satin
Richard Williams, *Guardian*

Overstatement can work – if it is vivid and specific. Here is the American journalist Dave Barry explaining 'Why Women Can't Play Baseball':

> Because, faced with the choice of rescuing a drowning baby and catching a high fly ball, a woman wouldn't hesitate to save the baby, even if the game was tied and there were men on base.

SENTENCES AND PARAGRAPHS

Start with the short sentence. That is: start by learning to write the short one, then practise adding longer ones to create contrast. Like this.

The impact of a short sentence is greater if it comes before or after a long one or several long ones. Here's a short sentence ending a paragraph:

> It was on the morning of day three that I started to worry about George and Rose. We were tramping through the African bush, dutifully scanning the wilds for primeval monsters, when I suddenly noticed that George was wearing Bugs Bunny socks. *And Rose had floral shorts.* [My italics]

And here's the next par – starting with a short sentence:

> *Even worse, they were talking loudly.* The great issue burning in their brilliant minds, as I tried to savour the incandescent glory of the African landscape, was this . . . [My italics]
> *Daily Telegraph*

In both sentences and paragraphs the key points are the beginning and the end. As with the piece as a whole, you must get the reader's attention and then keep it. Try to begin and end with a strong word or phrase.

In general, above all with features, vary the length of your sentences. There is a place for a series of *short* ones – if you want to produce a breathless or staccato effect because what you're reporting is dramatic or terrible. Here, for example, is part of a quote from the fire brigade:

> 'The cottage is now completely gutted. Everything has gone. Only the walls are standing.'
> *Daily Telegraph*

But there is no sense in writing a series of *long* sentences – unless your plan is to send the reader to sleep. Here, for example, is a paragraph of 71 words in just two sentences:

> Ministers, and those they employ to whinge on their behalf, are now given to complaining that the media pay far too little attention to their achievements over the first year in office. It's an example of this Government's hypersensitivity, not to mention the ferocious rivalries within it, that I and other colleagues have been contacted by Cabinet Ministers and their functionaries over the past week with check-lists of their personal triumphs.
> *Observer*

Political analysis seems to attract pompous and long-winded writing. In this case the sentences are long and complicated partly because the writer can't resist the aside, the parenthesis:

> Ministers, and those they employ to whinge on their behalf, . . .

> . . . hypersensitivity, not to mention the ferocious rivalries within it, . . .

Complete sentences, like words and phrases, are often written in threes to produce a rhetorical effect:

> Who were these people who sought to tell me what a good sunset is? Why were they invading my holiday? And how dare they defile my dusk?
> *Daily Telegraph*

FIGURES OF SPEECH

Alliteration, metaphor, simile and the rest* are part of vivid effective writing. But they can be overdone. The pun, for example, is a virus that gets into the computer systems of some tabloids.

Alliteration can be addictive. The local paper reporter who referred to 'Battersea's boxing brothers' (see page 20), which is straightforward, might not be able to resist the temptation of 'Clapham's cricketing cousins', which is clumsy and self-conscious.

---

* See *English for Journalists* for definition and illustration of the common figures of speech.

And what about the *Telegraph* travel feature writer quoted above? Does his 'how dare they defile my dusk' work as a phrase? There's something awkward and forced in the combination of 'defile' and 'dusk'.

Remember that alliteration – like other forms of repetition – can be unintentional. So sometimes you need to remove it from your copy to maintain an appropriate tone, to stop a serious piece sounding comic.

AVOID TOO MANY BUTS

'But' is a powerful word. Like 'and', it has its place in journalism whether in the middle of sentences or at the beginning. But you must not overdo it.

First, avoid the false 'but', often put in to revive a flagging sentence or paragraph. Second, avoid a succession of 'buts'. Even if some of them are 'however' or 'although', the effect is to leave the reader feeling giddy. For a 'but' changes the direction of the paragraph.

> The householder could, of course, search for the owner and arrange a deal. *But* tracing an owner is a long, laborious and frustrating task *although* local history may give some leads. Usually, it is when no-one comes forward with a paper title (title deeds), that householders technically squat. *But* it can be extremely frustrating . . . [My italics]
> *Ideal Home*

Too many 'buts'.

THE IMPORTANCE OF CONTENT

A word of caution to add to this emphasis on techniques and tricks: beware of putting colour into copy in an artificial way. Style, as was said early on in this chapter, is not a matter of adding embellishment to content. It is a matter of expressing content in a lively, vivid, pleasing way.

Faced with the (usually false) choice between style and content, many great stylists would in fact choose content. Here is that caustic wit Dorothy Parker, famous for her put-downs, reviewing the autobiography of the dancer Isadora Duncan:

> *My Life* . . . is a profoundly moving book. [Isadora Duncan] was no

writer, God knows. Her book is badly written, abominably written. There are passages of almost idiotic naivety and there are passages of horrendously flowery verbiage. There are veritable Hampton Court mazes of sentences. . . . There are plural pronouns airily relating to singular nouns but somehow the style of the book makes no matter. Out of this mess of prose come her hope, her passion, her suffering.

New Yorker

READ, ANALYSE, PRACTISE, POLISH

To develop your writing style, you need good models. We have tried in this book to provide some examples of the kind of journalistic writing we think you should read and try to emulate.

Look for well-written books by journalists – whether collected pieces or sustained reporting. *Homage to Catalonia* shows George Orwell at his best, reporting on the Spanish Civil War. Tom Wolfe's anthology *The New Journalism* has been quoted; there are good collections by the English interviewer Lynn Barber and the American ideologue P J O'Rourke; Ian Jack's *Before the Oil Ran Out* and Bill Bryson's *Made in America* are both worth reading.

We also suggest that you read widely outside journalism: history, biography, novels. Besides the writers already mentioned – Hemingway (everything), Tom Wolfe again (particularly *Bonfire of the Vanities*), Norman Mailer (*The Naked and the Dead*), Martin Amis (*London Fields, Money*) – we would recommend Graham Greene (*The Power and the Glory, Brighton Rock, The Quiet American*), Evelyn Waugh (*Decline and Fall, Scoop*), P G Wodehouse (the Jeeves–Wooster books), Carson McCullers (*The Member of the Wedding, The Heart Is a Lonely Hunter*), Patricia Highsmith (the Ripley books), Peter Carey (*Oscar and Lucinda, Jack Maggs*), William Boyd (*A Good Man in Africa*), Kurt Vonnegut (*Slaughterhouse-Five*), Margery Allingham (*The Tiger in the Smoke*), Alison Lurie (*The War Between the Tates*) and Sebastian Faulks (*Birdsong*).

Second, you need to go further than mere reading. You need to analyse the pieces you read and admire, and find out for yourself how they work. We suggest you follow the approach used in this book, naming and listing different types of intros and endings, for example. Does one of them contain a technique or trick you could use in your next piece?

Third – the most obvious point – you need all the practice you can get. With it, though, you need feedback.

If you work in the kind of office where copy just disappears into a black hole with never a word from anybody about how good or bad it is, you must try to get some reaction from other people – if not colleagues in the office, friends outside it.

Finally, polish: revise your pieces, and continue to revise them even after they've been published. Go back after a while and see how they could have been improved.

When you re-read something you've written, play the sub-editor: try to read it as a bored or hostile reader would. As we said earlier, try reading your copy out loud – ideally to a friend or colleague, otherwise to yourself. This way, you're likely to spot many of the errors and problems – repetition, awkward phrasing, obscurity. You could even read your copy into a tape-recorder, then play it back.

Always remember that you are writing for your reader not yourself. So be on the lookout for those fine phrases that seem brilliant at two in the morning but lose their shine the next day. If, as advised, you find yourself having to murder your darlings, they die in a good cause.

On the other hand, if you can make your writing lively, vivid, colloquial – and clear – you will serve your reader well and encourage them to keep coming back for more.

Glossary of terms used in journalism

ABC: Audit Bureau of Circulation – source of circulation figures
advertorial: advertisement presented as editorial
agony aunt: advice giver on personal problems sent in by readers
artwork: illustrations accompanying copy
ascender: portion of lower-case letter that sticks out above the x-height
attribution: identifying source of information or quote

back bench (the): senior newspaper journalists who make key production decisions
backgrounder: explanatory feature to accompany news story
banner (headline): one in large type across front page
bill: poster promoting newspaper, usually highlighting main news story
bleed: (of an image) go beyond the type area to the edge of the page
blob par: extra paragraph introduced by blob/bullet point
blurb: another name for standfirst or similar displayed copy
body copy: the main text of a story as opposed to headings, intro, etc.
body type: the main typeface in which a story is set
bold: thick black type, used for emphasis
breaker: typographical device, such as crosshead, to break up text on the page
broadsheet: large-format newspaper such as *The Times*
bust (to): (of a headline) be too long for the space available
byline: name of journalist who has written the story

calls: routine phone calls by reporters to organisations such as police and fire brigade
caps: capital letters
cast off (to): estimate length of copy
catchline: single word identifying story typed top right on every page
centre (to): set (headline) with equal space on either side
centre spread: middle opening of tabloid or magazine
chapel: office branch of media union

character: unit of measurement for type including letters, figures, punctuation marks and spaces

chequebook journalism: paying large sums for stories

chief sub: senior journalist in charge of sub-editors

city desk: financial section of British newspaper (US: home news desk)

clippings/clips: press cuttings

colour piece: news story written as feature with emphasis on journalist's reactions

context par: paragraph in feature providing necessary background, often linking intro with what follows

contacts book: a journalist's list of contacts with their phone numbers

copy: text of story

crop (to): cut (image) to size

crosshead: occasional line(s) of type usually bigger and bolder than body type, inserted between paragraphs to liven up page

cut-out: illustration with background masked or cut to make it stand out on the page

cuts: press cuttings

dateline: place from which copy is filed, usually abroad

deadline: time by which a journalist must complete story

deck: one of series of headlines stacked on top of each other

delayed drop: device in news story of delaying important facts for effect

descender: portion of lower-case letter that sticks out below the x-height

deskman: American term for male sub-editor

diary (the): list of news events to be covered; hence an off-diary story is one originated by the reporter

diary column: gossip column

direct input: transmission of copy direct from the journalist's keyboard to the computer for typesetting (as opposed to the old system in which printers retyped copy)

display type: type for headlines, etc.

doorstepping: reporters lying in wait for (usually) celebrities outside their homes

double spread: two facing pages

downtable (subs): those other than the chief sub and deputies

drop cap: initial letter of story or paragraph set in large type alongside first few lines of text (cf. raised cap: large letter raised above text)

dummy: 1 photocopied or printed (but not distributed) version of new publication used for practice and discussion; 2 blank version of established publication, for example, to show weight of paper; 3 complete set of page proofs

edition: version of newspaper printed for particular circulation area or time

editorial: 1 leading article expressing publication's opinion; 2 matter that is not advertising

em, en: units of measurement for type – the width of the two letters m and n

embargo: time before which an organisation supplying material, e.g. by press release, does not want it published

exclusive: claim by newspaper or magazine that it has a story nobody else has

face: type design

feature: article that goes beyond reporting of facts to explain and/or entertain

file (to): transmit copy

fireman: reporter sent to trouble spot when story breaks

flatplan: page-by-page plan of magazine issue

flush left or right: (of type) have one consistent margin with the other ragged

fount: (pronounced 'font' and sometimes spelt that way) typeface

free: free newspaper

freebie: something useful or pleasant, often a trip, supplied free to journalists

freelance: self-employed journalist who sells material to various media

freelancer: American term for freelance

full out: (of type) not indented

galley proof: typeset proof not yet made up into a page

gutter: space between pages in centre spread

hack/hackette: jocular terms for journalist

hanging indent: set copy with first line of each paragraph full out and subsequent lines indented

heavy: broadsheet newspaper

house style: the way a publication chooses to treat matters of detail, e.g. abbreviations

imprint: name and address of publisher and printer

indent: set copy several characters in from left-hand margin

in-house: inside a media organisation

input (to): type copy into computer

insert: extra copy to be included in existing story

intro: first paragraph of story

italics: italic (sloping) type

journo: jocular term for journalist

justified: type set with consistent margins

kill (to): to drop a story; hence 'kill fee' for freelance whose commissioned story is not used

knocking copy: story written with negative angle

layout: arrangement of body type, headlines and illustrations on the page
leader: leading article expressing publication's opinion
leading: (pronounced 'ledding') space between lines (originally made by inserting blank slugs of lead between lines of type)
leg: column of typeset copy
legal (to): check for legal problems such as libel
lensman: American term for male photographer
lift (to): steal a story from another media outlet and reproduce it with few changes
linage: (this spelling preferred to lineage) payment to freelances by the line
listings: lists of entertainment and other events with basic details
literal: typographical error
lobby (the): specialist group of political reporters covering the House of Commons
lower case: ordinary letters (not caps)

make-up: assembly of type and illustrations on the page ready for printing
masthead: newspaper's front-page title
must: copy that must appear, e.g. apology or correction

newsman: American term for male reporter
nib: news in brief – short news item
night lawyer: barrister who reads proofs for legal problems
nub par: paragraph explaining what a feature is essentially about

obit: obituary
off-diary: *see* diary (the)
off-the-record: statements made to a journalist on the understanding that they will not be reported directly or attributed
on spec: uncommissioned (material submitted by freelance)
on-the-record: statements made to a journalist that can be reported and attributed
op-ed: feature page facing page with leading articles

page proof: proof of a made-up page
par/para: paragraph
paparazzo/i: photographer(s) specialising in pursuing celebrities
paste-up: page layout pasted into position
pay-off: final twist or flourish in the last paragraph of a story
pic/pix: press photograph(s)
pica: unit of type measurement
pick-up: (of photographs) those that already exist, which can therefore be picked up by journalists covering a story
piece: article

point: 1 full stop; 2 standard unit of type size
proof: trial impression of typeset matter to be checked
proofread (to): check proofs
puff: copy that praises uncritically and reads like an advertisement
pull-out quotes: short extracts from feature set in larger type as part of page layout
pyramid: (usually inverted) conventional structure for news story with most important facts in intro

query: question mark
quote: verbatim quotation
quotes: quotation marks

range left or right: (of type) have one consistent margin with the other ragged
reverse out: reversal of black and white areas of printed image
roman: plain upright type
RSI: repetitive strain injury attributed to over-use and misuse of computer keyboard, mouse, etc.
run on: (of type) continue from one line, column or page to the next
running story: one that is constantly developing, over a newspaper's different editions or a number of days

sanserif: a plain typeface (with no serifs)
scoop: jocular word for exclusive
screamer: exclamation mark
sell: another name for standfirst, often used in women's magazines
serif: small, terminating stroke on individual letters/characters, hence serif type
setting: copy set in type
shy: (of headline) too short for the space available
sidebar: self-contained section accompanying main feature
side-head: subsidiary heading
sketch: light-hearted account of events, especially parliamentary
slip: newspaper edition for particular area or event
snap: early summary by news agency of important story to come
snapper: jocular term for press photographer
snaps: press photographs
spike: where rejected copy goes
splash: tabloid's main front-page story
splash sub: sub-editor responsible for tabloid's front page
spoiler: attempt by newspaper to reduce impact of rival's exclusive by publishing similar story
standfirst: introductory matter, particularly used with features
stet: ignore deletion (Latin for 'let it stand')
stone sub: sub-editor who makes final corrections and cuts on page proofs

story: article, especially news report

strap(line): introductory words above main headline

Street (the): Fleet Street, where many newspapers once had their offices

stringer: freelance on contract to a news organisation

sub: sub-editor – journalist who checks, corrects, rewrites copy, writes head-lines, captions, etc., and checks proofs; on newspapers, but not on most magazines, subs are also responsible for layout

tabloid: popular small-format newspaper such as the *Sun*

taster: production journalist who checks and selects copy

think piece: feature written to show and provoke thought

tip: information supplied, and usually paid for, whether by freelance or member of the public

tot: triumph over tragedy, feature formula particularly popular in women's magazines

typo: American term for typographical error

underscore: underline

upper case: capital letters

vox pop: series of street interviews (Latin: *vox populi* – voice of the people)

widow: line of type consisting of a single word or syllable

wob: white on black – type reversed out

x-height: height of the lower-case leters of a typeface (excluding ascenders and descenders)

Further reading

Dates refer to the most recent known edition.

PRACTICAL JOURNALISM

Aitchison, James, *Writing for the Press*, Hutchinson, 1988
Albert, Tim, *Medical Journalism*, Radcliffe Medical Press, 1992
Bagnall, Nicholas, *Newspaper Language*, Butterworth/Heinemann, 1993
Boyd, Andrew, *Broadcast Journalism*, Butterworth/Heinemann, 1993
Bromley, Michael, *(Teach Yourself) Journalism*, Hodder & Stoughton, 1994
Chantler, Paul, and Harris, Sam, *Local Radio Journalism*, Butterworth/
    Heinemann, 1993
Clayton, Joan, *Journalism for Beginners*, Piatkus, 1992
—— *Interviewing for Journalists*, Piatkus, 1994
Davis, Anthony, *Magazine Journalism Today*, Butterworth/Heinemann, 1988
Dick, Jill, *Freelance Writing for Newspapers*, A & C Black, 1991
Dobson, Christopher, *Freelance Journalism*, Butterworth/Heinemann, 1992
Evans, Harold, *Newsman's English*, Heinemann, 1972, out of print. (Also by
    Evans in the same series: *Handling Newspaper Text, News Headlines, Picture
    Editing, Newspaper Design*, all published in 1972; all out of print.)
Giles, Vic, and Hodgson, Frank, *Creative Newspaper Design*, Butterworth/
    Heinemann, 1990
Goldie, Fay, *Successful Freelance Journalism*, Oxford University Press, 1985
Greenwood, Walter, and Welsh, Tom, *McNae's Essential Law for Journalists*,
    Butterworth, 1997
Harris, Geoffrey, and Spark, David, *Practical Newspaper Reporting*, Butterworth/
    Heinemann, 1993
Henessy, Brendan, *Writing Feature Articles*, Butterworth/Heinemann, 1993
Hodgson, Frank, *Subediting: Newspaper Editing and Production*, Butterworth/
    Heinemann, 1987
—— *Modern Newspaper Practice*, Butterworth/Heinemann, 1992
Hoffman, Ann, *Research for Writers*, A & C Black, 1992
Hutt, Alan, and James, Bob, *Newspaper Design Today*, Lund Humphries, 1988
Jones, Graham, *Business of Freelancing*, BFP Books, 1987

Keeble, Richard, *The Newspapers Handbook*, Routledge, 2nd edition, 1998
Keene, M., *Practical Photojournalism*, Butterworth/Heinemann, 1993
Moore, Chris, *Freelance Writing*, Robert Hale, 1996
Niblock, Sarah, *Inside Journalism*, Blueprint, 1996
Sellers, Leslie, *The Simple Subs Book*, Pergamon, 2nd edition, 1985
Spiegl, Fritz, *Keep Taking the Tabloids*, Pan, 1983, out of print
—— *Media Speak/Media Write*, Elm Tree Books, 1989
Waterhouse, Keith, *Waterhouse on Newspaper Style* (replaces *Daily Mirror Style*, now out of print), Viking, 1989
Wilby, Peter, and Conroy, Andy, *The Radio Handbook*, Routledge, 1994
Wilson, John, *Understanding Journalism*, Routledge, 1996

ENGLISH USAGE AND STYLE

The classics

On usage the standard texts are Fowler and Gowers; on style Quiller-Couch and Middleton Murry. There is also a famous essay by George Orwell and an American gem, Strunk and White.

Burchfield, Robert, *The New Fowler's Modern English Usage*, Clarendon, 1996
Fowler, H W, *The King's English*, Oxford University Press, 1931
Gowers, Ernest, *The Complete Plain Words*, revised by Bruce Fraser, Penguin, 1987
Murry, J. Middleton, *The Problem of Style*, Oxford University Press, 1922, out of print
Orwell, George, 'Politics and the English Language', in Sonia Orwell and Ian Angus, eds, *Collected Essays, Journalism and Letters of George Orwell*, vol. IV, Penguin, 1970
Quiller-Couch, Arthur, *On the Art of Writing*, Cambridge University Press, 1919, out of print
Strunk, William, and White, E B, *The Elements of Style*, New York: Macmillan, 1979

The moderns

Many of the books listed below are by journalists. Particularly recommended are Bryson and Phythian (a distinguished schoolteacher). Lanham is a spirited attack on the classics.

Aitchison, James, *Dictionary of English Grammar*, Cassell, 1996
—— *Guide to Written English*, Cassell, 1996
Blamires, Harry, *Correcting your English*, Bloomsbury, 1996
Bryson, Bill, *The Penguin Dictionary of Troublesome Words*, Penguin, 1984
Crystal, David, *Who Cares about English Usage?*, Pelican, 1984
Dummett, Michael, *Grammar and Style for Examination Candidates and Others*, Duckworth, 1993

Fieldhouse, Harry, *Everyman's Good English Guide*, Dent, 1982, out of print
Greenbaum, Sidney, and Whitcut, Janet, *Longman Guide to English Usage*, Penguin, 1996
Hicks, Wynford, *English for Journalists*, Routledge, 2nd edition, 1998
Lanham, Richard A, *Style: An Anti-Textbook*, Yale University Press, 1973
Partridge, Eric, *Usage and Abusage*, Penguin, 1973
Phythian, B A, *Concise Dictionary of Correct English* (replaces *Teach Yourself Good English and Teach Yourself Correct English*), Hodder & Stoughton, 1993
Silverlight, John, *Words*, Macmillan, 1985, out of print
Vallins, G H, *Good English, Better English, The Best English*, Pan, 1963, out of print
Waterhouse, Keith, *English Our English*, Viking, 1991
Weiner, E S C, and Hawkins, J M, *The Oxford Guide to the English Language*, Oxford University Press, 1984
Whale, John, *Put It in Writing*, Dent, 1984
Wood, F T, Flavell, R H, and Flavell, L M, *Current English Usage*, Macmillan, 1981

HOUSE STYLE

Bryson, Bill, *Penguin Dictionary for Writers and Editors*, Viking, 1991
Grimond, Joe, *The Economist Pocket Style Book*, Business Books, 1991
Inman, Colin, *The Financial Times Style Guide*, Pitman, 1994
Jenkins, Simon, ed., *Times Guide to English Style and Usage*, Times Books, 1992
Macdowall, Ian (compiler), *Reuters Handbook for Journalists*, Butterworth/ Heinemann, 1992
The Oxford Dictionary for Writers and Editors, Oxford University Press, 1981
The Oxford Writers' Dictionary (paperback version of *The Oxford Dictionary for Writers and Editors*), Oxford University Press, 1990

NON-FICTION BY JOURNALISTS

This section includes collections and books about journalism.

Let Us Now Praise Famous Men is classic reporting from the 1930s about three Alabama share-croppers – impoverished cotton farmers. *The Years with Ross* is a memoir of *New Yorker* editor Harold Ross.

Agee, James, and Evans, Walker, *Let Us Now Praise Famous Men*, Houghton Mifflin, 1991
Amis, Martin, *The Moronic Inferno*, Penguin, 1987
Barber, Lynn, *Demon Barber*, Viking, 1998
Bernstein, Carl, and Woodward, Bob, *All the President's Men*, Pocket Books, 1994
Bryson, Bill, *Made in America*, Minerva, 1995
Carter, Angela, *Nothing Sacred*, Virago, 1982

Coleman, Nick, and Hornby, Nick, *The Picador Book of Sports Writing*, Picador, 1997

Evans, Harold, *Good Times, Bad Times*, Phoenix, 1994

Harris, Robert, *Selling Hitler*, Arrow, 1996

Jack, Ian, *Before the Oil Ran Out*, Fontana, 1988

Mitford, Jessica, *The Making of a Muckraker*, Quartet, 1980, out of print

O'Rourke, P J, *Holidays in Hell*, Picador, 1989

—— *Parliament of Whores*, Picador, 1992

Orwell, George, *Homage to Catalonia*, Penguin, 1989

—— *The Collected Essays, Journalism and Letters of George Orwell*, vols I–IV, Sonia Orwell and Ian Angus, eds, Penguin, 1970

Silvester, Christopher, ed., *The Penguin Book of Interviews*, Viking, 1993

—— *The Penguin Book of Columnists*, Viking, 1997

Terkel, Studs, *Working*, Penguin, 1985

Thurber, James, *The Years with Ross*, Penguin, 1963, out of print

Wolfe, Tom, and Johnson, E W, *The New Journalism*, Picador, 1990

REFERENCE FOR REVIEWERS

Art

Murray, Peter and Murray Linda, *The Penguin Dictionary of Art and Artists*, Penguin, 7th edition, 1997

Osborne, Harold, *The Oxford Companion to Art*, Oxford University Press, 1970

Books

Drabble, Margaret, ed., *The Oxford Companion to English Literature*, Oxford University Press, 5th edition, 1998

Sturrock, John, ed., *The Oxford Guide to Contemporary Writing*, Oxford University Press, 1996

Dance

Clarke, Mary, and Crisp, Clement, *London Contemporary Dance Theatre: The First Twenty-One Years*, Dance Books, 1988

Koegler, Horst, ed., *The Concise Oxford Dictionary of Ballet*, Oxford University Press, 2nd edition, 1982

Film

Katz, Ephraim, *The Macmillan International Film Encyclopedia*, Macmillan, 2nd edition, 1994

Walker John, ed., *Halliwell's Film and Video Guide*, HarperCollins, 13th edition, 1998

Music

Broughton, Simon, Ellingham, Mark, Muddyman, David and Trilloe, Richard, eds, *The Rough Guide to World Music*, The Rough Guides, 1994
Clarke, Donald, ed., *The Penguin Encyclopedia of Popular Music*, Viking, 2nd edition, 1998
Sadie, Stanley, ed., *The New Grove Dictionary of Music and Musicians*, Grove, 1997

Opera

Harewood, Earl of, and Peattie, Anthony, eds, *The New Kobbé's Opera Book*, Ebury Press, 11th edition, 1997

Television

Gambaccini, Paul, *Television's Greatest Hits: Every Hit Television Programme Since 1960*, Network Books, 1993
Hayward, Anthony, *Who's Who on Television*, Boxtree, 1998
Vahimagi, Tise, *British Television: An Illustrated Guide*, Oxford University Press, 1996

Theatre

Hartnoll, Phyllis, *The Oxford Companion to the Theatre*, Oxford University Press, 4th edition, 1983

Index